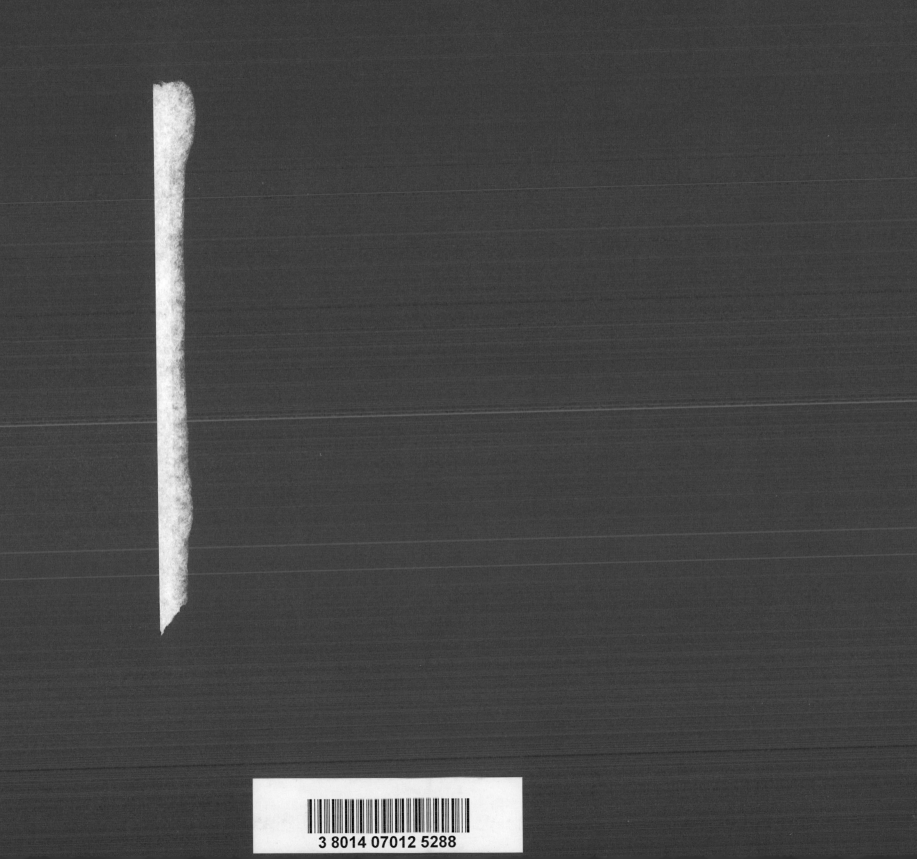

RED ARROWS

THE ROYAL AIR FORCE AEROBATIC TEAM IN ACTION

Photography and text by

JAMIE HUNTER

TOUCHSTONE
BOOKS LTD

First published in 2009 by Touchstone Books Ltd

Copyright © Touchstone Books Ltd 2009

Touchstone Books Ltd, Highlands Lodge, Chartway Street, Sutton Valence, Kent ME17 3HZ, United Kingdom. www.touchstone-books.net

A copy of the CIP data for this book is available from the British Library upon request.

The rights of Jamie Hunter to be identified as the author of this work have been asserted in accordance with Section 77 of the Copyright, Designs and Patents Act of 1988.

Photography by Jamie Hunter unless otherwise credited
Designed by Sue Pressley and Paul Turner
Edited by Philip de Ste. Croix

© British Crown Copyright/MOD images on pages 12 (top left) and 91 are reproduced with the permission of the Controller of Her Majesty's Stationery Office.

Printed and bound in Italy

ISBN: 978-0-9551020-9-7

◎ ROYAL AIR FORCE RED ARROWS™

The Royal Air Force Red Arrows logo is a registered Trade Mark of The Secretary of State for Defence and is used under licence.

Red Arrows has been produced with the full support of the Royal Air Force Aerobatic Team to give an overview of today's modern Red Arrows. Author and photographer Jamie Hunter has been given exclusive access to the team, to enable him to obtain exciting and previously unpublished imagery and to portray the values, skills and professionalism of the RAF. www.raf.mod.uk/reds

Previous page: A stunning break shot of 'Gypo' high above the clouds over RAF Scampton.

Right: A deep blue summer sky is punctuated by the Red Arrows' distinctive coloured smoke trails.

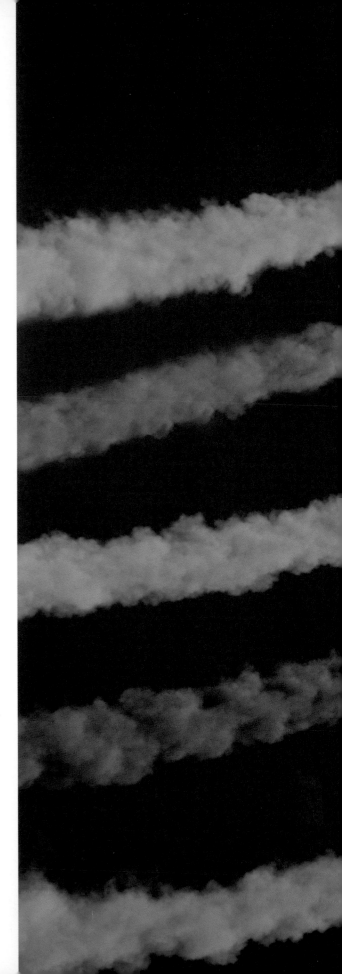

CONTENTS

The Red Arrows
Foreword by Air Chief Marshal Stephen Dalton CB BSc FRAes FCMI RAF

6

Introduction
Wing Commander Jas Hawker, Red 1

8

'Smoke On, Go!'
The Red Arrows in action

22

'Reds, Rolling…Now!'
The Reds' evolution

42

The Diamond Nine
The pilots

52

'Holding the Bank'
The support team

88

'Roll, Go!'
The Hawk aircraft

108

'Letting It Out'
Behind the scenes

124

'Gypo Going Full'
The display

146

'Reds, Break, Break…Go!'
Appendices

170

The Red Arrows

Air Chief Marshal Stephen Dalton CB BSc FRAes FCMI RAF

Above: Air Chief Marshal Stephen Dalton

Over the last 90 years the Royal Air Force has adapted continuously to meet changing demands and has conducted air operations wherever and whenever the nation has called. Technological and operational agility have been fundamental to delivery of the capabilities inherent in military air power. The airmen and women who fly, service, direct and support operations are, however, the key to the Service's success; it is their bravery, dedication, agility, professionalism and commitment to excellence that makes the Royal Air Force 'second to none'!

The Royal Air Force Aerobatic Team (RAFAT) – the Red Arrows – is the epitome of this excellence and has earned the team an unrivalled international reputation. Their characteristically dynamic flying displays have inspired and thrilled the public (and professional aviators) around the world for nearly 45 years. The iconic signature formation of the Diamond Nine is recognised universally as that of the 'Reds' and the attention to detail, the precision of the flying, the quality of the aerobatics and the formation changes are the visible demonstration of the skill and agility of the team.

The personnel who make up the Red Arrows are a microcosm of the Royal Air Force. The pilots are proven combat aviators who have completed operational tours on Harriers, Tornados or Jaguars. The aircraft are meticulously maintained and prepared to the highest standards for each and every flight by dedicated, focused and highly capable engineers who themselves have served with distinction and to great effect on the RAF's frontline. Whilst behind the scenes the Public Relations and Administrative staff, many of whom are drawn from the Royal Air Force's support branches and trades, work tirelessly to enable the Red Arrows to be at their best for each and every display, .

This book celebrates the immense contribution of the men and women who have served on the team, whether as the Reds, Blues, Circus or behind the scenes. It clearly shows that the Royal Air Force men and women who serve on the RAFAT can, and will, maintain the Red Arrows' reputation for precision, skill, commitment and excellence for many years to come.

Stephen Dalton

Opposite above: The early morning sun silhouettes one of the team's Hawks during the first training sortie of the day (left). The team flies the famous Vertical Break during a display (centre). In the cockpit: the display is dynamic and dramatic – these pilots are some of the best on the planet (right).

Opposite below: Wg Cdr Jas Hawker, Red 1, leads the team over the top of a loop.

Introduction

Wing Commander Jas Hawker, Red 1

In 1965, under the leadership of Flt Lt Lee Jones, seven Folland Gnat training aircraft and crews were formally established as the full time Royal Air Force Aerobatics Team – the Red Arrows era had begun. The skills displayed by the Red Arrows have roots that can be traced right back in the history of the RAF and the Royal Flying Corps. Flying your aircraft to its limits is vital in combat, with formation flying being important in bringing maximum firepower safely on to a target in the shortest possible time. Combining these two qualities – the finest aircraft handling with precision formation keeping – has been the trademark of the Red Arrows in its distinguished history and one that every 'ex-Red' is justifiably proud of.

I have the privilege of being the 18th leader of the Red Arrows and although the personnel and aircraft have changed since 1965, the ethos of the team is unaltered; our motto of 'eclat' meaning 'brilliance' is at the forefront of everything that we do. The RAF is unique in requiring the team leader to have previously served a three-year tour as a wingman on the team. I was fortunate enough to have been originally selected to join the Red Arrows in 1999 and during that three-year tour I flew in the Synchro Pair and experienced some of the most demanding and exhilarating flying possible. Then in October 2006 I returned as the team leader for a second incredible period with the team. I never thought it was going to be easy, but I think that I can speak for every pilot who has ever donned a red flying suit by saying that it is by far the most demanding job they have ever done. On the ground, now more than ever, my entire Squadron has an important ambassadorial role to play, representing the RAF and the 'Best of British' not only around Europe, but worldwide.

It is, however, in the air where the true hard work is done. There is no room for complacency and the trust placed in the skill of your fellow team pilots has to be 100 per cent when flying at 400mph only 300ft above the ground and with wingtips only feet apart. The Red Arrows are world-class and reaching that level does not just happen by chance.

> *" ... flying your aircraft to its limits is vital in combat ..."*

I take some of the finest fighter pilots in the RAF and then put them through the most rigorous of training programmes, flying three times daily, five days a week. Under constant scrutiny, it requires the utmost dedication, hard work and commitment to reach the demanding standard that is expected by the RAF and the British public.

Throughout the past 45 years the pilots, ground crew and support staff of the Red Arrows have been called upon to demonstrate the exceptional standards expected of the Royal Air Force Aerobatic Team and the wider RAF across the world, flying over 4170 displays in 53 countries. I hope that the truly unique photographs and descriptive commentary included in this book give you an insight into the spectacular world of the Red Arrows.

Jas Hawker.

Previous pages left: Smoke on ... GO! The world-famous Red Arrows appear in spectacular style as they begin a display, arriving above the crowd trailing their trademark red, white and blue smoke.

Previous pages right: In the cockpit with team leader Wg Cdr Jas Hawker (left). The Boss, Wg Cdr Hawker, briefs the team before another summer display (centre). Wg Cdr Hawker shares a joke with Corporal Darren Budziszewski (right).

Leading from the front

Wg Cdr Hawker clearly has one of the most sought-after and demanding jobs in the world as team leader of the Red Arrows – surely every schoolboy's dream job. Every working day he leads the team and their nine bright red Hawk jet trainers around the sky as they paint the heavens with coloured smoke in a graceful display of aerial perfection. The leader's famous radio call of 'Smoke on... GO!' is surely one of the most evocative and famous phrases in modern aviation. As Red 1 his responsibilities are huge, with the role of the formation leader being absolutely critical to the display. The 'Boss' (as he is known by his squadron) is responsible for positioning and timing throughout the complex routine and for maintaining the exceptionally high standards expected.

In addition to the rigours of display flying and practising, the Officer Commanding the Red Arrows must also lead the whole squadron. The job has been described as being similar to that of a chief executive of a medium-sized company. Red 1 is responsible for a squadron of 100 people who strive to represent the best that the RAF has to offer. As well as having total responsibility for the flying aspects of the job, he is also responsible for the welfare and well-being of all other members of the Red Arrows and their families.

Left: Sweeping across RAF Scampton, the view from Red 1 as the team performs a summer In Season Practice (ISP).

Above: Wg Cdr Jas Hawker.

Right: The gleaming Hawk of the Red Arrows team leader. Flt Lt Charlotte Fenn is the Junior Engineering Officer on the team in 2009 and she supports the leader and his aircraft on the road during the display season.

Opposite: Charity work is extremely important to the Red Arrows, with numerous good causes and trusts working closely with the team. Here the 2008 team members pose with a charity mascot.

> "... Jas flew with the team for the 2000-2002 display seasons ... in 2009 he marked his third year as Team Leader ..."

Wing Commander Jas Hawker

Wing Commander Jas Hawker was educated at The Castle School in Thornbury, near Bristol. Whilst at school Jas was a member of his local Air Training Corps and gained an RAF Sixth Form Scholarship. He joined the RAF immediately after completing his A-Levels. After training, his operational flying career began on the Tornado GR1 ground attack aircraft. He was then posted to instructional duties on the Tucano T1 trainer and became the RAF's solo Tucano display pilot for the 1997 display season. Eager to return to the frontline, he recommenced operational flying duties on the Tornado GR4 at Royal Air Force Bruggen in Germany.

After a successful application to join the Red Arrows, Jas flew with the team for the 2000-2002 display seasons, during which he was selected to fly in the Synchro Pair. On leaving the team he returned to the Tornado GR4, this time as a flight commander on No 31 Squadron at RAF Marham.

During his RAF career, Jas has been involved in military exercises all over the world and recent operations in the Middle East. He has amassed well over 4500 flying hours to date. In 2009, at the age of 38, he marked his third year as Team Leader and Officer Commanding The Red Arrows, having taken command in October 2006.

Jas is married to Cath and they have two children, Jess and Molly. His hobbies include all water sports, especially kite-surfing and windsurfing, golf, occasionally playing the piano and taking his English Pointer dog on long walks. He is a proud supporter of Tottenham Hotspur FC.

WG CDR JAS HAWKER
FLT LT CHARLOTTE FENN

Previous pages left: Red 4 concentrates hard on the Boss as the team sweeps into a climb and the Palm Tree split at the end of the first half of the display.

Previous pages right: The team leader flies a smooth and accurate line that allows the other team members to concentrate on him. During the first half of the routine the pilots all fly their formation 'off' the leader.

Left: The Diamond Nine loop starts to split for the 'Spaghetti Break' – a tricky but impressive manoeuvre that splits the team into equal spacing ready for landing.

Opposite: The Diamond Nine loop seen from above as the team loops. Looking down through the formation the shadow of the smoke shows on the water below.

Following pages left: In their element, two Reds perform inverted during the display.

Following pages right: Picture perfect, the team places huge emphasis on precise formation flying. The Red Arrows are very critical and work hard to make sure they are inch perfect.

Left: *The team flies Big Vixen formation as they flash impressively above the waves.*

Opposite above: *'Roll Go!' The team rolls as a formation, led by Red 1 (left). The coveted red flying suit of Red 1, the Boss, Wg Cdr Jas Hawker (centre). The concentration shows as Wg Cdr Hawker 'gets in the zone' and prepares mentally for the rigours of the display (right).*

Opposite below: *The Red Arrows have flown the Hawk T1 trainer since 1979.*

ACTION

'Smoke On, Go!'

The Red Arrows in action

'Ladies and gentlemen, the Red Arrows!' Everyone has heard of the Red Arrows, most people have seen a Red Arrows display or caught a fleeting glimpse of them as they fly around the UK, but just how does everything come together to make for such an incredible aerial spectacle? How can such a marvel that makes crowds gasp, flinch and even cry be achieved safely and executed with such precision time and time again? So many factors have to come together with such precision that the very concept of the team is as impressive as the final polished display itself.

Many people don't actually realise that the Red Arrows are part of the Royal Air Force. They are the main public face of the RAF and the team's reputation is something the Service is immensely proud of. The 'Reds' are renowned throughout the world as ambassadors for both the RAF and the United Kingdom as a whole, having completed over 4170 displays in 53 countries. However, the team is far more than nine pilots in red flying suits flying nine red jets. The famed pilots are supported by an equally dedicated support team that fulfils a diversity of tasks to ensure the show goes on year after year.

Today, some 40 per cent of the RAF's assets and 5000 of its 41,000 personnel are serving overseas on operations around the world, with the RAF being at the forefront of defending UK interests and of international peace and security. Many of the Red Arrows' pilots and support staff have recently returned from Afghanistan and Iraq and some will be temporarily detached on operations overseas during their time with the Red Arrows. And once they leave the team, all will return to duties which directly support the RAF's operational commitments around the world.

The nine Red Arrows display pilots are drawn from RAF fast jet squadrons and serve a three-year 'tour' on the team. These pilots will have flown Tornado GR4, Tornado F3, Harrier GR9, Jaguar or Eurofighter Typhoon aircraft. They apply for selection to make it into the team. For this they must have notched up a minimum of 1500 flying hours

and completed a tour on a frontline squadron and been assessed as above average in their flying role.

The nine display pilots are numbered Reds 1-9 and each will fly in one particular position for a whole season before moving to a new position. The number is always applied to the same position. So, for example, Red 1 is always the leader, Red 2 is always on the right-hand wing of the leader, and so on back to Red 9 at the rear of the formation. A pilot that has his first year as Red 2 will then move to another position – moving to the Red 4 slot, for example. Reds 1-5 form the front section of the formation and are collectively known as 'Enid'. Reds 6-9 are known as 'Gypo', with the famous Synchro Pair being part of this as Reds 6 and 7. The Synchro Pair perform the highly popular and breathtaking opposition crossover manoeuvres during the second half of the display sequence, with Red 6 fulfilling the roles of both 'Gypo' and Synchro Leader.

Previous pages left: The team flies in Kite formation during the first half of the display that showcases a variety of different sweeping nine-aircraft formations.

Previous pages right: The team primes its smoke with a quick blast on the runway. This helps them to check wind direction as well as preparing the smoke system. It also makes for an impressive pre-take off spectacle (left). 'Ladies and gentlemen… The Red Arrows'. Red 10 announces the arrival of the team (centre). Flypasts and display arrivals are flown in Big Battle formation (right)

The support team

It is the hard work of the team's support personnel that keeps the Red Arrows flying. The support team is made up of a Team Manager, a Road Manager (also known as Red 10), a Public Relations Manager and officer (the only two civilians on the team), two Engineering Officers, an Adjutant and approximately 85 engineering technicians and other support staff. The latter are known as 'The Blues' (they wear distinctive royal blue flying suits during the display season), and they represent nine of the RAF's broad range of over 65 technical and non-technical trades. Every team member has undergone intensive training in their particular specialisation throughout their RAF careers.

The teamwork shown by the pilots in the air is reflected in the dedication and professionalism of the support staff on the ground. Every single member of the team puts in incredibly high work rates, often working long and unsociable hours 'behind the scenes' in order to keep a hectic schedule on track in roles ranging from engineering to logistical support and public relations work.

The Red Arrows are directed by the RAF Events Team at RAF Cranwell in Lincolnshire which has responsibility for allocating all RAF display assets. All bids for Red Arrows displays must be submitted by September each year for shows taking part in the following year. Members of the Events Team will then discuss with each of the RAF display teams which displays must be carried out and which displays are operationally feasible. Display venues can also be influenced by the requirements of the RAF recruiting organisation. It may wish to target a particular area and

views a display by the Red Arrows as positive aid to encouraging young people to consider a career in the RAF.

Charity work and fundraising forms a large part of the team's non-flying activities and they have achieved great success over the years. In addition to the intense flying schedule, the whole team is constantly involved in charity and community work – representing the RAF at home and around the world. Everyone in the Red Arrows team has a vital role to play and clearly everyone works with huge professionalism and pride.

Left: The famous Synchro Pair flies dynamic crossover manoeuvres in the second half of the display.

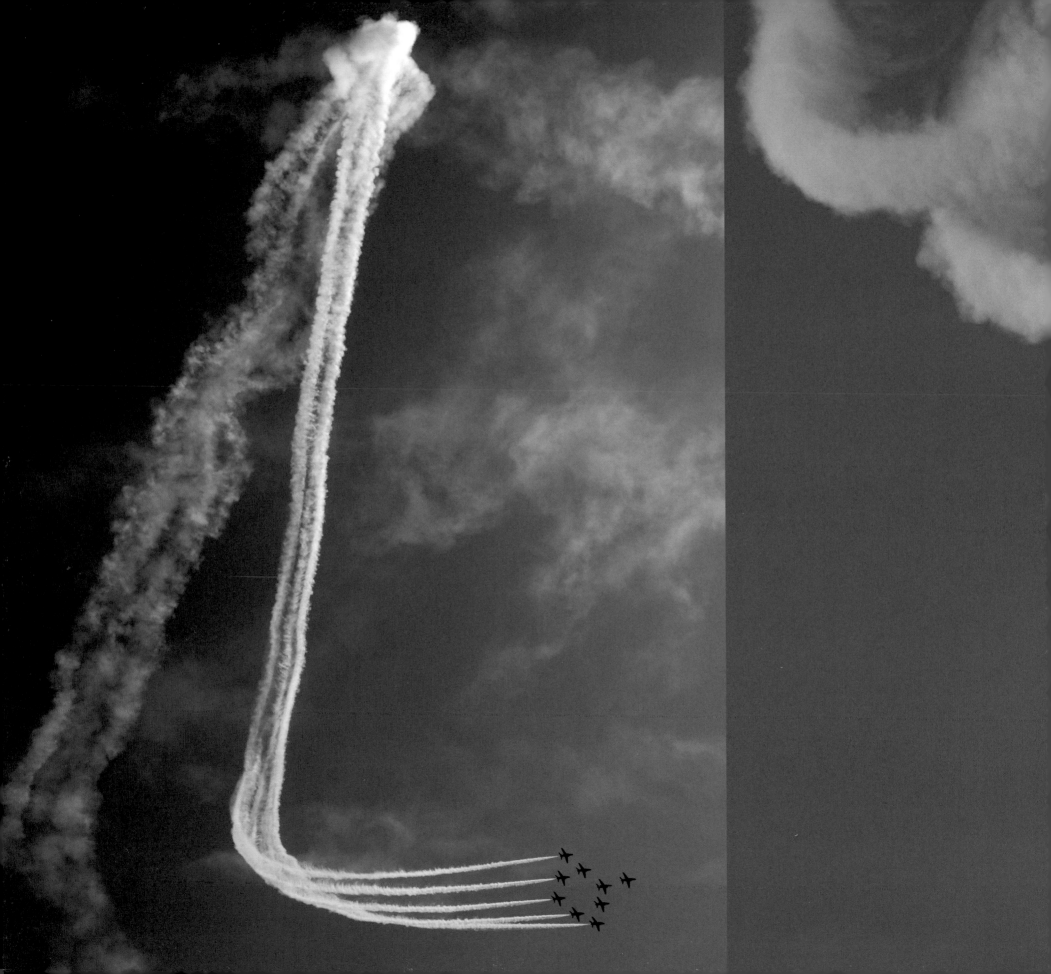

Above: *The view over the head of Red 7 as 'Gypo' get airborne behind 'Enid' for the start of the display.*

Opposite: *'Gypo' is the name given to Reds 6, 7, 8 and 9. The second half of the display sees these members of the team perform some of the most famous manoeuvres including inverted formation flying, crossovers and breaks. In 2008 'Gypo' was led by Flt Lt Pablo O'Grady, seen here breaking towards the cameraship aircraft flown by Red 10 Flt Lt Andy Robins.*

"... everyone in the Red Arrows team works with huge professionalism and pride ..."

Previous pages left: *Often the team changes formation at the top of a loop. An impressive feat! The team enters this loop in Swan formation and emerges in Kite, a manoeuvre known as the Swan to Kite loop and twist.*

Previous pages right: *Enid formation, lead by Red 1, flies the Helix.*

Above: Seen from Red 8, Reds 6 and 7 sneak around the back of the display centre as they prepare for the 'Mirror Roll'. Some of the most demanding parts of the show go on behind the scenes as the team positions for the next element of the display.

Right: Pulling past the vertical during a summer display.

Above: *Flying a perfect down-line, the pilots have total faith in the team leader as they follow his jet and strive to achieve the ideal position relative to his aircraft.*

Left: *The view from Red 1 as the team flies the Palm Tree split, with Reds 3, 5 and 9 breaking away with exact spacing.*

Above: Looping high above Cyprus. The Red Arrows deploy every spring to RAF Akrotiri in Cyprus to finely hone the display in the clear Mediterranean skies.

Right: With home base RAF Scampton in the background, the team practises in typically dull British weather.

Previous pages left: From the ground the formation looks graceful and effortless. It's a different story in the air as the team puts every ounce of effort into getting it just right.

Previous pages right: The smoke from a jet further ahead in the formation masks the sun as Red 7 tucks in tight. Often, the smoke stains the aircraft's fins as they fly through the other aircraft's jetwash.

Above: *Which way up? Red 6 captured against the sun with Red 8 in the background during the Mirror Roll.*

Left: *Diving out of a loop the eight other pilots in the formation chase the Boss.*

Opposite above: The team flies with just feet between the wingtips (left) – this is close formation flying! Even upside down, with eyeballs seemingly wanting to pop out, the team flies very close (centre). Those Synchro Pair crossovers really are as hair-raisingly close as they look (right).

Opposite below: The famous lines of a Red Arrows Hawk, Red 6 photographed from Red 7 during the Mirror Roll.

Right: The tank under the fuselage of the Hawk stores the dye and diesel that produces the famous smoke.

Previous pages left: The team flies the Phoenix Bend, with Reds 5 and 9 trailing blue smoke, and red smoke coming from Reds 4 and 8. Each formation and manoeuvre involves a specific smoke plan.

Previous pages right: The Synchro Pair break for the camera with the remaining seven aircraft formating in the background.

Following pages: The impressive Vertical Break (left). The team goes over the top of a loop in Kite (centre). Smoke trails swirl in jet vortices as the Synchro Pair break for action (right).

'Reds, Rolling...Now!'

The Reds' evolution

The 1950s and 1960s were the heyday of RAF jet aerobatic display teams. By the mid-60s almost every Flying Training School, and several operational squadrons, had their own teams. The RAF then decided to form a single, full-time professional team. In 1964 the Red Pelicans were formed flying six Jet Provost T4s to represent the RAF. The same year a team of five yellow Folland Gnat jet trainers also formed the Yellowjacks at No 4 Flying Training School at RAF Valley in north Wales, led by Flt Lt Lee Jones. The following year he was posted to the Central Flying School (CFS) to form the Red Arrows. The Royal Air Force Aerobatic Team (RAFAT), the formal name of the Red Arrows, began life at RAF Fairford in Gloucestershire, then a satellite Station of CFS. The Red Arrows name derived from a combination of two earlier teams names, the famous Black Arrows and the Red Pelicans.

In their first season, 1965, the seven Red Arrows pilots flew 65 displays in Britain and around Europe. The following year two spare pilots were added to the team, but the Reds continued to display just seven jets. However, it wasn't long before seven became nine on a temporary basis and the first display with nine aircraft occured in July 1966 for the benefit of HRH The Duke of Edinburgh. The practice of carrying spare pilots proved unsatisfactory because the display was so specialised that each position had its own demands. To be of any use at all, the spare pilots had to be capable of filling any position at very short notice. Thus, they required more training than any other member of the team and, as a result, became more skilled. Not surprisingly the spares became dissatisfied with their roles as reserves. The Red Arrows flew nine aircraft in displays from time to time from mid-1966 onwards, but it was not until 1968 that the team was officially increased to nine aircraft.

The team took delivery of British Aerospace Hawk trainers in the autumn of 1979 and that winter converted from the Gnat, working up with the new Hawks for the 1980 display season. The team's 4000th display was at RAF Leuchars Battle of Britain Airshow in September 2006.

Right: The Red Arrows flew the Folland Gnat jet trainer from 1965 to 1979. These two examples are not actual ex-team aircraft but are painted in the representative Gnat-era team schemes by their civilian owners, including Chris Hudson, seen here flying his aircraft.

Right: One of the most famous of all Red Arrows pilots, Ray Hanna joined the team in its first year. Becoming team leader for the following four seasons, Hanna was renown for his incredible flying skills as the bright red Gnats cemented the team's reputation.

Previous pages left: Red flying suit, white flying helmet … the best of the best.

Previous pages right: In 2007 the Red Arrows applied new Royal Air Force logos to its Hawks (left). The Reds represent the highlight of summer air displays at a variety of popular venues around the UK and Europe (centre). In 2004 the Red Arrows marked the team's 40th display season. Here, a Gnat jet trainer sits alongside the team's current line-up of Hawks at RAF Cranwell (right).

Above: Flt Lt Charlie McIlroy takes time out for a rare photograph during the display season. He flew with the team from 1985 to1987.

Charlie McIlroy: Recollections

Every once in a while I am reminded of a time over 20 years ago when I enjoyed what was simply the best flying job in existence. One such incident occurred last summer on a bright sunny day. My wife Marie, our boys and I were out with some friends cycling in the Peak District on a Saturday afternoon when the air was suddenly filled with the noise of approaching jets at low level. Looking up we saw 10 red Hawks in two loose formations on their way to a show somewhere. Everyone around us had stopped to look and kids were pointing at the aeroplanes with excitement. I looked at my wife Marie and she had a look that was a mixture of excitement and sympathy on her face. 'You used to do that!' Indeed I did, but as I have mentioned already, it was some while ago.

The memories now are a bit of a kaleidoscope of people, places and planes. I do remember the formal interview in 1983 at Scampton that was part of the selection process for admission into the team. I was under the impression at the time that it would be a fairly informal affair with the team leader and the Commandant CFS. When I entered the room I was somewhat taken aback to see at least seven people seated behind a long table, including a psychiatrist. There was one solitary chair in front of the table. I made the best of marching up to the table and saluted. 'Can you please close the door Charlie' was the first thing that was said to me. I marched back down the room to the door, which closed by itself just as I was reaching for it. Things were not going well. For the next 30 minutes I made a complete idiot of myself and I

still writhe with embarrassment at the memory. I did not get selected that year.

The following year though, after a lot of preparation and practice interviews, I was successful and I was selected to join the team. When I joined the Reds almost 25 years ago in the late summer of 1984 it would have been difficult to imagine that the team would be still be in existence today, and indeed be flying the same aircraft a quarter of a century later. That they do is testament to the Hawk as an outstanding aeroplane and also to the fact that the Reds are now an intrinsic part of British culture.

Life in the fast lane

Life on the Red Arrows was very different from a regular RAF squadron. Despite being very demanding, the work up was conducted in a mature and calm atmosphere at a pace to suit everyone. When problems arose, solutions were sought with a 'can do' attitude. The pressure to perform well in the air was obviously there but I never felt under pressure from other members in the team.

In my first week, Simon Bedford, who was Red 4, took me aside and told me, 'Make sure you enjoy the next three years because it is going to pass very quickly'. Three years later, after more than 1200 training sorties and transit flights and over 360 displays in 29 different countries, it was all over and I was back in a green flying suit. Over time the memories of that time have faded and merged somewhat, but there were moments, incidents and places that still remain extremely vivid in my mind.

28 August 1987, Sydmouth Bay, Devon

One minute to go, the Boss calls us into 'big vic' formation as we begin our run in. There are only a few scattered clouds and it's perfect conditions. 'Smoke on...GO!'. The crowd flashes past underneath as we arrive spot on time. 'Pulling up...Diamond...GO!' The air is full of aircraft changing position. Red 7 Ade Thurley and I move quickly into line astern on the lead where we remain for most of the next ten minutes as all nine aircraft perform a series of loops, rolls and wing overs. It is my third year and as Red 6, Synchro Leader, I am directly behind the leader, concentrating on keeping my distance and depth correct in relation to his aircraft. I remember the intensity of the training for Synchro. I would often fall asleep for an hour as soon as I got home.

There are small changes required for the different formations, Apollo was flown very tight, Wine Glass more relaxed, and as the speed of the formation varies the forces on the control column change constantly. The change to Concorde requires only that I stay in line astern on the Boss, but when it comes, it is as if the leader, Red 7 and myself are suddenly accelerating through the rest of the formation – a strange illusion as it is actually the rest who decelerate on either side of us. Throughout the first half of the show both Red 7 and I catch glimpses of the display site. Coming down the backside of a loop the sea is a perfect turquoise blue, out of the Delta Roll we get a look at the cliffs opposite the crowd line – spotting the rocky peninsula that we will use for positioning. The display is going well and the responses to the leader's radio calls are enthusiastic and loud. Acknowledgement calls of 'Eight!', 'Nine!' from the respective pilots, sharp and succinct. It was a kaleidoscopic mixture of blue sky and sea, green fields, the beach, crowds and red aeroplanes.

Synchro time

As we enter the second half of the show Red 7 and myself split from the formation, we pull up and once in the vertical, each of us rolls through 90 degrees and arcs over, red smoke trailing to form the Heart. The next seven minutes are fast and furious and demand total concentration. Our speeds vary between 120 and 380 knots and at times we are pulling over 7G, occasionally pushing negative 3.5G making our eyeballs feel as if they are going to pop out. We alternate our Synchro Crossovers with a pass by the main formation, each time we finish a manoeuvre we clear the display line and fly away behind the crowd. Timing is everything; we fly precise patterns at exact speeds and make adjustments for the wind. Running back in we both cross the top of the cliffs for the next pass. I am acutely aware of the huge crowds on the cliff tops, we dive down to 100ft over the waves for another crossover – each time I hear the noise of Ade's jet as we pass head on a few metres apart with a closing speed of over 800mph. We roll out and, reaching the end of the crowd line, we break hard upwards towards the crowds on the cliff tops rolling onto our backs as we pass over them.

Getting the line right is easy over a runway but over the sea it is much more of a challenge. Timing the pull up for our rolling pass is purely down to our eyes, a second too early or late means being over 350 metres too close or far apart. Today is good, watching Ade arcing towards me I know the pass is going to be good. Once more I hear his engine as he passes above me in height but below the belly of my own aircraft while I am inverted. Pulling hard towards the crowds on the cliff tops, I can see people waving frantically above me, to the side and then below as I roll again. We reverse our turns and dive down as the whole formation runs in for the finale join up loop. We have lots of overtake and slide in deep from the sides of the formation as the team reforms as the Diamond Nine. Judicial use of airbrakes and manoeuvre gets rid of the overtake and we slide into position in time for the Bomb Burst. The leader calls the split and the formation of nine aircraft rolls apart and each pilot dives out to nine separate points of the compass. My line takes me down a narrow valley to the rear of the crowd. I try not to be too much of a hooligan on the pull out!

Minutes later we are on the ground at Exeter airport. I reflect on the past 30 minutes and glance at Ade, who looks over with a big grin on his face. The reason I remember this display so vividly is because it was one of only a handful of performances in three years where I felt totally satisfied that the show had gone exactly to plan. In all the rest of the practices and shows there was always something that we felt we could have improved upon. Striving constantly for total perfection is both extremely demanding and difficult to achieve.

Opposite: The team trails a sweeping arc of smoke as they fly in Big Vixen formation.

Amazing experiences

The airshow at Bex in Switzerland also stands out, flying around the Alps in stunning scenery before diving down into the valley for the display. The air was crystal clear and the mountains appeared very close – in fact there seemed to be a lot more ground than sky during that particular show, which got the adrenalin pumping. One particular Saturday we spent over an hour flying in formation with a British Airways Concorde trying to get a perfect picture, culminating with a formation flypast over the *QE2* in the English Channel.

We went on tour to the Far East in the summer of 1986, a terrific time that provided us with some amazing flying experiences. One of the highlights of that tour was meeting King Hussein of Jordan. We flew a display for him at Amman, where the altitude and the high temperature made for difficult conditions. We were presented to His Royal Highness immediately after the display. I was drenched in sweat and looked as if I had climbed out of a swimming pool. The king was an extremely dapper gentlemen but seemed quite happy to shake the hand of this sweaty officer who was dripping all over his expensive carpet.

Next we went to Egypt and I remember they were obsessed with security and would not provide us with any maps to help us plan the show. They were, however, more than happy for us to get airborne bristling with cameras for a photoshoot over the Pyramids. At the culmination of that display I had the pleasurable experience of finding myself perfectly lined up for a low pass down their flightline that was packed with brand new Mirage 2000 fighters. We were

all in turn presented with a large coin-shaped memento by the head of the Egyptian Air Force. These were in small spring-loaded cases. I flipped mine open 'Beam me up Scotty'. The coin tumbled out and rolled across the floor in a long curve back around the top man and then clattered down some steps making a terrific noise.

A royal audience

On a number of occasions we were visited by royalty. We displayed for HRH The Queen Mother and we were presented to her afterwards. She was a charming lady who really seemed to appreciate the show. However, I was furious to discover afterwards that due to an intervening concrete pillar, the official photographer failed to get a picture of me shaking hands with Her Royal Highness. The resulting photograph with which I was presented shows what appears to be the Queen Mother with her hand stuck in a pillar with me nowhere to be seen.

Most of all I remember the intensity of constantly trying to achieve perfection. On leaving the team I

Above: The 2004 team led by Sqn Ldr Spike Jepson celebrated the 40th anniversary of the formation of the Red Arrows. The team are seen here with the Air Chief Marshal Sir Jock Stirrup, Chief of the Air Staff, and Air Marshal Sir Joe French.

Opposite: The team practises every year in Cyprus, working through the new season's routine over the sea near RAF Akrotiri. The deployment has proved popular over the years and gives a great opportunity for the whole team to prepare for the forthcoming season.

managed to persuade the powers that be that they needed me to fly the Harrier as opposed to the Lightning that I had previously flown before joining the team. The Harrier looked like a good challenge to move onto and I went on to serve with both Nos 3(F) and 4(AC) Squadrons. Many people ask if, after flying with Red Arrows, other flying is mundane. I answer that tearing across the Nevada desert at 100ft, flat out, with seven other Harriers during a Red Flag exercise is far from mundane!

Life after the Reds

After 17 years of service in the RAF, I felt it was time for a change and I followed many other previous Red Arrows pilots into commercial aviation. I joined Cathay Pacific Airways in 1993. Being the Captain of a large commercial airliner still provides challenges and a lot of job satisfaction. However, eventually the question: 'Do you miss flying upside down?' got the better of me and I had to admit I did. In fact I was missing it all so much that I started looking for opportunities in light aviation. I got an instructor's rating and now, as often as I can, I fly an Extra 300 competition aerobatic aircraft with Ultimate High at Kemble airfield.

Looking back, what I miss about the team are the people. Membership of the team is a very unique experience. Sometimes it feels like a dream, did I really do that? It was and always will be, without doubt, the highlight of my flying career. I also know that every time I see the Red Arrows I am going to experience a mixture of feelings. Not least of those is a yearning for times past.

Right: On several occasions throughout the 2004 display season a civilian-owned Gnat made frequent flypasts with the team to mark the 40th anniversary of its formation. The red Gnat was usually flown by RAF test pilot Wg Cdr 'Willy' Hackett or former team member Andy Cubin piloting a Gnat in 'Yellowjacks' colours from Delta Jets at Kemble.

Right: One of the team Hawks taxies out for a display at RAF Waddington Airshow in 2004.

Opposite above: The Royal International Air Tattoo in 2007 saw the Red Arrows, lead by Wg Cdr Jas Hawker, perform a flypast with three Spitfires and a Hurricane to mark the 50th anniversary of the RAF Battle of Britain Memorial Flight. The Hurricane and three Spitfires were the original four aircraft operated by the BBMF (Battle of Britain Memorial Flight). One of these is now owned and operated by Rolls-Royce.

Opposite below: The Royal Air Force Aerobatic Team of 2009. Incredibly, six of the original Hawks that first joined the team in 1980 are still flying with the Red Arrows.

The Diamond Nine

The pilots

Red flying suit, bright red Hawk jet trainer, flying at 300ft in front of thousands of spectators, surely being a 'Red Arrow' is one of the coolest jobs on the planet? It is as close as any pilot today can get to the heady days of the 1950s when British test pilots such as John Derry and Neville Duke were national heroes.

Every year nine Royal Air Force fast jet pilots are privileged to call themselves 'Red Arrows'. Despite what some people might lead you to believe, these pilots are not prima donnas and they aren't elitist, they are thorough professionals, who know that they are under constant scrutiny as they represent the RAF. They are personable, totally approachable, friendly, generous and under no illusion that they are role models to so many people. They are also among the best pilots in the RAF.

As a spectator, the display always looks so effortless, the pilots are so relaxed, so confident. The pilots all have total trust in one another, total faith in the leader as they chase him around the sky – as he makes the finest of

adjustments to ensure the formation is always perfectly on its mark, on time, its symmetry exact as if welded together. It is a manifestation of perfection that the team prides itself upon.

Every year a long list of RAF fast jet pilots apply for the three slots that will be available for the following season with the team. This is narrowed to a shortlist of nine applicants who are then examined during a thorough selection period at RAF Akrotiri in Cyprus, known as 'shortlist week'. They are subjected to a gruelling flying test, formal interview and peer assessments. The completion of shortlist week is followed by the existing team members going into a highly secretive closed meeting in the Officers' Mess. Here, the three successful pilots are chosen. Only those who have excelled themselves will have made it. The Boss gathers feedback from all members of the team and they exit the meeting knowing the big news – who's in and who hasn't made the grade.

Previous pages left: Flt Lts Mike Ling, Simon 'Kermit' Rea and Damo Ellacott work through pre-display briefing notes before a show.

Previous pages right: Sqn Ldr Graham Duff and Flt Lt Andrew 'Boomer' Keith listen intently during a briefing at RAF Scampton (left). The dark visor masks the intense concentration needed during a display (centre). Sqn Ldr Ben Murphy waves to the crowd as he taxies in after a display (right).

Left: Flt Lt Zane Sennett, Red 2 for the 2009 season: 'In gusty conditions you have to accept that the jets shift around a lot. Our task is to iron out the relative movement and resist the temptation to over control and exacerbate errors'.

Left: Sqn Ldr Graham Duff in 2009, proudly wearing his red flying suit. It is difficult to imagine just how much dedication, how much skill and how much determination is needed to earn one of these cherished flying suits.

Sqn Ldr Graham Duff: How I got in

"I first saw the Red Arrows at the Leicester Airshow when I was 12 years old. My stepfather and I had sat in the middle at the front of the show for the whole day and were about to go home, but the bloke next to us said we should stay for the finale of the Red Arrows. We did so only through politeness really. It quite literally knocked my socks off – they started with a Diamond Nine formation flypast over the crowd. That was the defining moment when I was inspired to be a fast jet pilot in the RAF.

I never thought I could be a Red Arrow, even during my time flying the Jaguar attack aircraft or teaching advanced flying in the Hawk at RAF Valley. I clearly remember once phoning my Mum during flying training while walking through the Officers' Mess at RAF Leuchars. I was very excited – the Red Arrows were in the ante-room and I'd just walked past them!

Around Christmas time each year the team puts out an advert to all RAF squadrons inviting applications from all the pilots who have the right qualifications. You need to be at least of Flight Lieutenant rank, have a minimum of 1500 hours flying fast jets and you must have been assessed as above average throughout your flying career. You must also have completed at least one operational flying tour (i.e. flown a frontline jet – all our pilots have seen active service, and when they finish their three years on the team will return to operations with the RAF). It takes about five years to get through all the RAF training to be a frontline pilot and about a further six to gain the flying hours.

So in January 2005 I found myself reading the application form and realising I had the right qualifications. With nothing to lose, I applied. One of the plus points of applying is you get invited for a day out with the team at RAF Scampton during the Red Arrows winter training, so the team can get to know who is applying and you get to know what you are letting yourself in for. I flew across to Scampton from RAF Valley for my day out and remember being very excited. So much so that I remember thinking that they must have thought 'who is this weirdo?' I recall asking the Executive Officer at the time, Sqn Ldr Dunc Mason, if he minded if I took a camera with me during the flight – very uncool for a wannabe Red Arrow. Needless to say that was the last I heard of that application.

Then the signal went out again the following year. I had been bitten by the desire and had figured out I must act more relaxed next time. Another thing in my favour was that the three new pilots who had got in the previous year were my friends. I had flown Jaguars with them and when they were about to join the team I made sure I was the guy at RAF Valley who would show them how to fly the Hawk again. So again I applied and again I went down for my day out in a Hawk from RAF Valley. I logged seven trips that day, one transit over to Scampton; five practice sessions sitting in the back with the team, and one transit back to Valley. I went to sleep early that night!

The team gets between 30 and 40 applications every year for the three places and nine candidates make it to Cyprus for shortlist week. This time I'd been a lot calmer and I was one of the lucky nine. I was to report to RAF Brize Norton in April for a week away with the team at

> *"... they started with a Diamond Nine formation flypast over the crowd. That was the defining moment when I was inspired to be a fast jet pilot ..."*

Opposite: *Sqn Ldr Graham 'Duffy' Duff in the cockpit of the Hawk as he prepares for a display. 'Duffy's' desire to join the Red Arrows stretches right back to his childhood.*

RAF Akrotiri. I instantly lost all that cool! I received a phone call from the then Red Arrows public relations manager, Rachel Huxford, saying that the BBC wanted to film a documentary on the Red Arrows shortlist week and the nine candidates. I was given the chance to opt out, but I remember Rachel saying, 'You do realise that the Red Arrows is the public face of the RAF and if you opt out it will look bad on your application...' OK, count me in.

Shortlist week

The shortlist started at Brize Norton and it was all very embarrassing pitching up in civilian clothes with a set of golf clubs and flying out on the same aircraft as a load of Royal Marines in combat gear going to Afghanistan. The only saving grace was that we'd all served in Iraq or Afghanistan at one time or another.

The BBC crew was in close attendance to record the whole event. My heart dropped when the lady asked for my passport, I hadn't even considered it. Passport? But this is a military flight! Heck, I might have failed already. Luckily the team manager was in attendance and managed to sort it for me and got some paperwork together to do the trick. I insisted the BBC didn't film the event. I had had a sense of humour failure and didn't want a camera in my face at my lowest point.

The shortlist week runs from Tuesday to Wednesday at Akrotiri and it involves three backseat passenger flights each day with the team during a full display practice, with each candidate aiming to fly in each of the nine formation positions before the end of the week. It also includes a round of golf on Saturday with the team. Monday sees more passenger rides and a formal interview, Tuesday involves a 10-minute flying test and on Wednesday the shortlist nine watch the display from a very good vantage point on the cliffs. Then it's time to head for home on a high and full of nerves leaving the team to sit down and choose their preferred three to join them.

There is an extensive social programme during shortlist week that is all aimed at testing your social skills when you are tired, under pressure and in demanding circumstances. It's difficult not to let your true character show by the end of the week – and that's the team's aim. It normally works the other way round – it is so hard to be yourself and not try to be the person you think they are looking for. Having seen it now from both sides, it is very obvious which people are relaxed and themselves as opposed to the people who are trying to be someone else and failing miserably.

All applicants must at least pass the flying test; this is graded and doing very well is a big plus. Of all the shortlist occurrences only failing the flying test will prevent you from applying again in future years. The flying test is quite daunting. As fast jets pilots we all do possess a level of formation expertise, but the way the Red Arrows do it is very different. The Red Arrows follow voice commands from the leader, importantly without pause, but the normal RAF fast jet method is to use your eyes and follow what you see. The difference is the onset of movement, slow for normal formation flying and very fast for the Red Arrows.

Left: Flt Lt Damo Ellacott checks his cockpit prior to joining the line of taxiing jets as they depart Scampton for a show weekend.

Also the Red Arrows fly very wide formations, up to nine aircraft across. To make the formation seem to move as one you simply cannot wait for movement to develop from the leader (the normal way of doing it) as you'd be left way behind. The far outside man has to start moving before the leader to stand any chance of keeping up so you must blindly move your control column on the leader's command before the leader moves his and hope you've done it right. If you haven't, or if the guy inside you hasn't, you're going to get very close (that is pretty much the key to the whole winter training – hence the mutual trust needed between each member of the team).

The critical flying test

The flying test is flown in the back seat of the executive officer – that year it was Red 8, Flt Lt Dave Slow. The Boss was Sqn Ldr Dicky Patounas and he led the two aircraft formation and flew a series of loops and rolls and positioning turns. Dave handled the take-off and landing portion and handed me the control for the rest.

I remember Dicky barking orders like 'tightening' or 'pulling up', but I didn't trust his voice command and was waiting for movement to develop before moving my aeroplane, meaning that I was left way behind as his aircraft disappeared off into the distance. Although it is only a 10-minute test, you have ample opportunity to make a complete fool of yourself.

Overall I don't think I fared too badly (you only find out at a later stage if you've failed, not how well you've done). I should have performed reasonably well as I was a current Hawk pilot and my job was teaching new Hawk pilots at the time. Reasonable flexibility is shown to each pilot. However, unsafe flying is a failure regardless of who it is. You have to feel sorry for the Tornado, Harrier and Typhoon pilots; they haven't been in a Hawk for some time and all aircraft fly very differently. During the flying test, either being perfect (not likely) or displaying a learning curve (getting better as you go) is the secret to passing. As many who saw the BBC documentary will know, I failed the formal interview spectacularly. The interview is

Opposite above: Team pilots' helmets sport a striking red arrow (left). Sqn Ldr Duff's helmet visor cover is typical in that it depicts the pilot's position in the diamond formation, this being Red 8 for 'Duffy' in the 2009 season (centre). Flt Lt Andrew Keith, known as 'Boomer', glances at his watch as he leaves climbing into the cockpit to the very last possible second. The pilots are always challenging themselves (right).

Opposite below: Flt Lt Simon 'Kermit' Rea climbs in with no time to spare during 'Springhawk' training at Akrotiri. The pilots take seconds to strap in and be ready for radio check in and engine start. It's not something to be late for.

conducted in front of the Boss, and two other senior officers in the Red Arrows command chain. Not my finest moment. I resolved to do better next year.

I went home in no doubt I had not done well. I was also one of those people trying too hard to be someone I thought the team wanted and not myself. I found the whole week a horrible experience, which is odd because in essence it is an all-expenses trip in Cyprus flying with the Red Arrows, which sounds perfect on paper. I was far too worried about each action I performed or thing I said and spent all my spare time worrying about what an idiot I was making of myself rather than just enjoying the experience.

A year later

So a year passed and I moved jobs to the Empire Test Pilot School (ETPS) at Boscombe Down. This was a fantastic job and I filled the one post at the school for a non-test pilot instructor pilot. Amongst my other responsibilities I was to offer an outside view of the flying they were doing and teach the new students how to fly various aeroplanes before they learnt the test pilot techniques. I got fully involved and over a year I flew 30 different types of aircraft, helicopters, multi-engines as well as fast jets, all from the front or captain's seat. Brilliant!

Then I got a phone call from Dicky Patounas in November. He said that I should apply again, but work on my interview technique. That was the only feedback I have ever got. For the team an unwritten rule is no one talks about what was said behind closed doors during the shortlist, even when you get on the team. I've tried;

"… during the flying test, either being perfect (not likely) or displaying a learning curve (getting better as you go) is the secret to passing …"

Left: *Looking out from Red 1 towards Reds 2 and 4. Reds 2 and 3 sit either side of the leader and have to be like rocks on his wings. The pilots are constantly making tiny correctional movements on the stick and throttle to stay in position.*

Opposite: *The Diamond Nine completes a perfect loop. The jets may be moving relatively to each other by several feet, so the pilots have to work very hard to maintain a perfect formation.*

Above: Lifting off the sun-bleached runway at RAF Akrotiri – the shadows show that precise formation positions are even adhered to on take off.

"... this time it went much better – it was all about the interview, and I aced it ..."

Opposite: Sqn Ldr Duff signs the Form 700 prior to a display. This means that he is taking responsibility for the jet.

'Here, have another drink, anyway what happened on my shortlist?' Nothing. Perhaps the only good thing about the BBC documentary for me was that I got to see just how bad my interview was, so I could learn and take advice from the 1.2 million people whom I've seen since then! So I re-applied.

This time round I didn't know the new Boss, Wing Commander Jas Hawker (pronounced Jase, he hates Jazz. It always draws a smile when a journalist introduces him incorrectly on national TV). I got shortlisted again and I was joined again by Flt Lt Simon 'Kermit' Rea who was also unlucky the year before and had featured in the BBC documentary. This time it went much, much better – it was all about the interview, and I aced it. I was also much more relaxed – the team all knew me, had seen me on a previous shortlist and still gave me an opportunity to come out to Cyprus again. That thought gave me the inner confidence I didn't have on my first shortlist. I also knew some guys who didn't get shortlisted that time and they were strong candidates, so things were looking good.

We arrived back in the UK on the Wednesday and at five o'clock on Friday afternoon I received a voicemail message on my mobile. I had missed the call as I had been flying. It was Flt Lt Mike 'Lingy' Ling, one of the two Tornado F3 pilots on the shortlist week. It was a fairly garbled message but I was pretty sure he said I had got in along with him and 'Kermit'. An obvious wind-up I thought, especially as I wasn't expecting to find out until at least the following week at the earliest. Just in case, I tried phoning my boss at ETPS; he was out. I tried phoning the

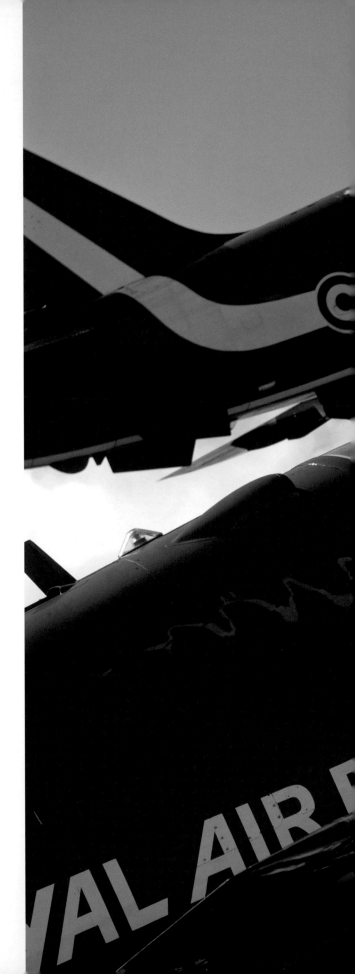

> *"… it still seems unreal. I find myself looking around the room thinking, wow, I'm in the same room as the Red Arrows … I count up to eight and realise that I am the ninth. Unbelievable!"*

Boscombe Down communications department, where the announcement would have arrived. Friday at five o'clock – no chance. So I phoned another guy from the shortlist, he hadn't heard. Lingy's phone was engaged, aargh!

I was just about winding myself up into a frenzy when I received a call from an unknown number. 'Hi Duffy it's Wing Commander Jas Hawker here. Have you heard?' I hadn't so I said 'No Boss, what?' I don't know why I called him Boss, because at that stage he wasn't. 'How do you fancy calling me Boss for the next three years?' 'Flippin heck, I'd love to!' 'Well done you're in. See you at Scampton soon'. And that was it. I was going to be a Red Arrows pilot.

The three of us FNGs (a friendly term for New Guys) got together with the team for a weekend at the Royal

International Air Tattoo in RAF Fairford in July and flew in the team's back seats during the show. I even heard the Radio 2 presenters talk about it on the Monday morning. I lay awake smiling and thinking I was in the back of what they were looking at. Then I started at RAF Scampton with the team in September 2007. We trained all winter until my first display in Beaumaris, on Anglesey, just near my old haunt of RAF Valley in May 2008.

Even now I'm in the team and have completed a display season, it still seems unreal. I find myself looking round the room thinking, 'Wow I'm in the same room as the Red Arrows,' I then count up to eight and realise that I'm the ninth. Unbelievable!

Right: Flt Lt Zane Sennett in Red 2 works hard to keep his position; 'Here you can see I am a little deep. I have to stop the error getting worse, hold my depth and then gradually melt back to my correct reference position. It is a smooth squeeze on the stick and you have to remember not to be too reactive and overcompensate'.

Winter training

When the team completes its summer display season in September it could be assumed that a nice break is on the cards. Not a chance. As soon as the season is over, the team bids farewell to outgoing team members at the annual End of Season Guest Night at RAF Cranwell and immediately begins training the new team for the following year.

The party at Cranwell is as spectacular as the display flying – full of pomp and pageantry – and is a welcome chance for the Reds to celebrate another successful year. However, it is only a brief respite before the whole squadron resets and readies for the new season. Back to work on Monday morning, the cherished red suits have been traded for standard green RAF flying suits and the team knuckles down for some serious training.

Above: Red 7's car parking spot at Scampton, with neatly manicured grass and the jets on the flightline in the distance.

Above right and right: The Boss, Red 1, Wg Cdr Jas Hawker briefs the team members carefully during winter training at Scampton. Every single element of the display, no matter how small, is briefed and debriefed in minute detail.

Left: Junior Engineering Officer Flt Lt Charlotte Fenn helps the Boss strap in before a display.

Wg Cdr Jas Hawker

"The biggest challenge over the 2007-2008 season was that the schedule for us was just non-stop. We completed the 2007 display season and then ran straight into a two-month tour of the Middle East and Far East. This was an amazing tour, but it dramatically reduced our 2008 season training time. We worked very hard to be ready for the 2008 season and then after getting our Public Display Authority (PDA) in May we went straight into another tour, this time to Canada and the USA. The tours are planned very carefully and the RAF is very mindful of not over-tasking us, but with pulls from defence industry and the need to represent the UK we are careful to ensure that everything we are asked to do is workable. The bottom line is that we want to take the display to as many people as possible; sadly we just can't physically do everything.

For the 2009 season we were back up to about 26 weeks of training, an additional five weeks over 2008. This meant that I was able to change a few elements of the display for the 2009 season – for 2008 I had to keep

it similar to the previous year. So we have some new manoeuvres, which is very welcome for us. The way that I fly the first half of the display is about as tight and as slick as possible now I think.

The weather has been a major factor for us in the last two seasons in the UK – indeed we were forced to cancel eight displays in 2008 – a lot more than normal. Interestingly, it is actually the transit flights to show venues that I lose sleep over. Leading a large formation of 10-11 aircraft around in poor weather is extremely challenging.

Displays in poor weather are relatively cast in stone; yes, the wind direction and terrain differ, but I am in a zone that I am very comfortable with. I get all the weather conditions from Red 10 on the ground as we run in for the display and I think about how the wind will affect the display. Quite often the wind is very different at 500ft than it is at 2000ft and 5000ft – so I have got to see what it is doing as we are making our first loop and judge where it is taking me. I am always thinking two manoeuvres ahead. If I was reacting to every loop or every bend I would be

constantly fighting to get back in the right place and the show just wouldn't flow correctly.

Learning the show

The display is learned very much as a building block process, putting it together in bite-size pieces before we link it all together. We fly the left-hand side of the display and then the right-hand side before we start to link it all together about the end of March. As we progress through winter training, we have started linking looping and rolling manoeuvres with each of the formation shapes where applicable, linking these together and building the formation. It is important to remember that none of us actually has the display written down in the cockpit. You simply can't do this job and look in the cockpit to see what is coming up next, so it's got to be absolutely ingrained in your head – more so than your wedding anniversary.

As we fly the routine I have got to make sure that every one of my control inputs is the same, I have to be very smooth. I have got everyone's safety to look after – in

Above: The view from Red 1 as 'Enid' performs the famous 'Rollbacks'. This involves Reds 2 and 3 or 4 and 5 performing a smart roll and slotting back into formation. The call comes from the Boss: '4 and 5…roll GO!'

the sky and on the ground. For the guys in the formation, their flying is actually probably more demanding and to do my job as leader without having flown 'down the back' of the formation would be incredibly difficult. I don't sit down at the beginning of the month and I say 'OK I would like to achieve this by here' or anything like that – there is no point pushing ahead if someone isn't able to cope with a manoeuvre. We tend to find that one person will find something easy that others will find a nightmare.

The other big factor is the great British weather. There is no point planning to fly loops and finding that

you have dense fog. Basically, I know where I want to be at the end of a particular week and I know the overall training requirements – I am almost like the conductor of an orchestra. Having done two years of the pre-season work up, it all seems a lot slower to me now as I enter my final season, but I know that my experience will mean that the coming year will be the tightest and best flown display under my tenure. 99

Right: The team frequently changes formation at the top of a loop. It is seen as a natural time to make such a change and to be ready to present the next shape in the subsequent manoeuvre. The aircraft have slowed to around 170mph at the top of a loop and so the reduced wind over the control surfaces makes the controls a little sloppy, meaning the pilots have to caress their jets into position.

"... always thinking two manoeuvres ahead ... I am almost like the conductor of an orchestra ..."

Right: *Changing formation is all about what the team calls 'cadence'. The pilots are moving positions in the formation, but all are flying their position off the leader, while having a peripheral view of some of the other jets in the formation. For example, the move to Concorde from Short Diamond starts with the radio call of 'Concorde GO!' from Red 1. This is followed by acknowledgement radio calls from Reds 2 and 3: 'two!', 'three!' and an ensuing metronomical count as the pilots whisper to themselves; four (airbrake out), five, six (airbrake in), etc. This means that all the aircraft move as one. Some may be dropping back into a space another jet is vacating, so to avoid backing into their team mates they use the 'cadence' count.*

Opposite: *Another show complete, Wg Cdr Hawker leads the team back to their parking spots.*

Striving for perfection

The three new pilots joining the team have a mountain to climb in terms of meeting the challenges that will be thrown at them – starting with winter training. They will have already been flying in the back seat during summer displays, but now it's time for them to embark officially on training.

The new pilots on the team are put right at the front of the formation for the first year, on the wing of the Boss. The process begins with small formations of three or four aircraft as the new pilots learn flying references and formation shapes, flying three times a day, five days a week. Each sortie is briefed thoroughly before it is flown and is recorded on video from the ground. After the pilots have landed, the sortie is debriefed in minute detail using the video footage. Slowly and safely, the display sequence is developed by the team. The Red Arrows will not generally fly together as a formation of nine aircraft until February, five months after training first begins.

The new display pilots for the 2009 season were Flt Lt Zane Sennett (Red 2), Flt Lt David Montenegro (Red 3) and Flt Lt Dave Davies (Red 4).

Above and below right: Flt Lt David Montenegro and the team emerge from briefing and head for the locker room. The Red Arrows' day is carefully timed and extremely hectic. Periods of intense flying are interspersed with a quick cup of tea and a snack, maybe some admin, and lots of briefings.

Flt Lt David 'Monty' Montenegro

" So far it's been terrific. My last Tornado F3 flight before I came to the team was in the Falkland Islands with No 1435 Flight on the frontline Quick Reaction Alert (QRA). I then came straight to the team for shadowing in September and October. My first impression was that it is fascinating just how many people you meet; everyone from the guys that service the jets to the Governer of Jersey.

The flying training is a nice build-up with a gradual learning curve initially, but once we started with a five-ship and then seven in the formation the workload really started to increase with new formation positions, a new dynamic break, it's absolutely fascinating. The quantity of flying we do is just incredible – averaging about 15 flights a week. That's a lot more than you expect on a frontline squadron so it's a real change of lifestyle.

At this point we have nailed the arrival sequence. We know it is a minute and a half sequence that includes three different formation positions. We all know that we are going to do a loop, a roll and two bends – so it's fairly easy to remember all that. The real difficulty is making sure that my control inputs are the same every time – so we maybe practise one particular element up to six times on a single sortie to make sure we all get the manoeuvre exactly the same. If the Boss's jet moves before yours does, you're already too late so we have to pre-empt his move – and we get our cue for this from his radio calls, which are so vitally important. So when he says 'Coming left now' I am already going on the 'n' of 'now'. That was one of the biggest factors to learn during initial training. Early on I

Left: Another display team roars overhead and does its best to disturb a team briefing during an airshow.

Below: Engines whining, the Hawk powers off its chocks and out to fly a practice in the specially restricted airspace above Scampton that the team makes such good use of.

was moving as the command finished – but that is too late. Now I am finding that I have moved at the right time and, guess what, I'm in the correct position.

Today we started flying the Swan formation. That involves Reds 2 and 3, Zane and I, flying line astern on the Boss in very close formation – less than half an aircraft's length between us. We have to use a lot of rudder control just to keep us from swinging out wide in turns or into the guys alongside us – it is very different from anything we've been taught before. The technique of having to keep wings matched and ruddering yourself in or out of position is a new skill. This means that if we go wide, we don't use a rolling input but a rudder input to correct it. This way our wing angles match and look neater, plus you don't 'wing flash' your team mates. "

Above: Sweeping low over the turf at RAF Shawbury. As well as public displays, the Red Arrows also entertain at the various private family days at RAF air stations.

Left: Flt Lt Zane Sennett enjoys a quick chat with the Boss about the forthcoming practice as they walk out to the jets during training on a crisp winter's morning; 'No Boss, I was down it in the move to Swan'. There's always a lot of chat about formation positions and any corrections needed.

Flt Lt Dave Davies

"This is very different formation flying from what I am used to. We teach new fast jet pilots a reactive technique, but here the Boss' voice commands are so important because otherwise we would get a huge ripple effect in the formation or a big bow. The farther out you are in the formation, the farther you have to manoeuvre – so you have to move earlier to keep it all matched. Reds 4 and 5 positions are said to be a little more demanding than 2 and 3 because of that – but because I was current on the Hawk, I got the Red 4 slot for my first season.

To keep our formation positions we each use references on other aircraft. My references as Red 4 depend on which formation we are in but the majority of the time I am flying to keep Zane's head on the Boss, that is how I keep in line. Red 8 outside me does the same, everyone else down the wing works off the first aircraft as references. We also use flap struts and other aircraft features as references but once Zane is squared on the Boss I am just going up and down a line. In the big formations I am flying 80 per cent of the time off the Boss as my reference, plus a little bit off Red 2 and Red 7."

Right: Silhouetted against the sun, the team loops over the clouds. Good weather and light winds means that the pilots' workload is more manageable.

"... the farther out you are in the formation, the farther you have to manoeuvre – so you have to move earlier to keep it all matched ..."

Left: *One of Red 2's roles is to hype up the team as they start a show. Flt Lt Zane Sennett, Red 2 for 2009: 'It's a chance for me to set the tone with a rousing phrase or a shout to the boys to crank it up to help get us fired up'.*

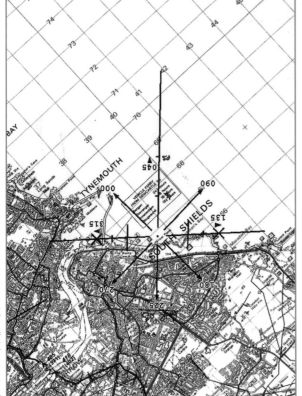

Above and above right: Synchro pilots plot the finer points of their routine on the display location 'pitch map'. These are drawn up and briefed in careful detail so the pilots can be familiar with turning points, landmarks, safety elements and areas to avoid.

Previous pages left: Sqn Ldr Ben 'Baz' Murphy climbs out of the Hawk after a Synchro Pair training sortie with Flt Lt Mike Ling.

Previous pages right: Having shut down after a training sortie, Sqn Ldr Ben Murphy monitors a minor snag in the cockpit as the engineers work to correct the issue.

Opposite: Flt Lt Pablo O'Grady and Sqn Ldr Ben Murphy, the Synchro Pair for the 2008 season, talk through the details of their forthcoming display.

The Synchro Pair

The Synchro Pair are Reds 6 and 7. For the 2009 season this is Sqn Ldr Ben Murphy and Flt Lt Mike Ling respectively. Red 6 is Synchro Leader and will have flown as Red 7 (Synchro 2) the previous year. For the initial phase of winter training the Synchro Pair work together independently of the rest of the team, building trust, learning the demands of their routine which plays a major part in the second half of the display when 'Enid' and 'Gypo' sections conduct more dynamic manoeuvres.

Flt Lt Mike 'Lingy' Ling

" When you first start on the team you are striving for perfection in the formation shape, so my first year was as Red 3. At the end of last season I was delighted to be selected for the Synchro Pair by the new Synchro Leader 'Baz' Murphy. So initially 'Baz' and I are not even looking at the formation parts of the first half. That will come later but our priority initially is our opposition work. It's all about making sure our manoeuvres look the same. The two of us are off on our own all the time to start with and hardly see the other chaps. We go off as a pair and the rest fly in their appropriate formations.

We started off our Synchro training flying up at 2000ft, but now we have worked down to our display height of just 300ft. My first 12 trips of training were just designed to work my base height down to 100ft, with Group Captain Nick Seward, Commandant Central Flying School (CFS), or 'Baz' observing me for safety. 'Baz' has very different control inputs to mine – so we are testing the matches. We have been fairly mismatched up to now. We have to make sure we get our smoke exactly level with the horizon, because any errors there can be very obvious.

Our first manoeuvre for the second half of the display comes off the break at the end of the nine-ship formation first half. This involves a crossing break at 8G, going away from each other for a Derry Turn and then we pull down towards our crossing point. We then apply full power and call 'threshold' when we are at the start of the opposite ends of the runway. We aim to cross at the mid-point of

the runway, but an error of timing can mean we are off our mark. Our work with the formation for the first half of the display mainly involves some line astern formations – down in the stem of the formation positions.

Our specific 'Gypo' manoeuvres involve bringing Reds 8 and 9 on board. This includes some very complex formations and manoeuvres and they have to be learnt in a stepped process. For example I have just started learning the Corkscrew Roll in. This involves 'Baz' and I being upside down in very close formation at only 300 feet above the ground and in its full form will see Reds 8 and 9 rolling round our smoke.

Flt Lt Andrew 'Boomer' Keith

For 2009 I am flying in the Red 9 position, and I am also the squadron 'Exec', second in command. I actually came to the RAF from the Royal New Zealand Air Force, having flown the A-4 Skyhawk. I initially flew the Harrier and completed a tour and a half on the front line. It was a pretty busy time. The first thing I was told when I joined the RAF was that I would go to war at some stage. I had come here to do operational flying so that was expected; indeed I completed four tours in Afghanistan with 'Happy' IV Squadron. In fact my last Harrier flight before I joined the Reds was in Afghanistan. I landed at Kandahar and then flew back to the UK and joined the team.

When I first came to the UK joining the Reds wasn't even on my radar. My initial exposure to the team came from guys who had been on the team and were back on the Harrier Force. They told me to get up here to Scampton

and fly in the back seat with the team. After three or so years I got to know the guys and I thought, actually this is a possibility. I got to shortlist week and that was great. I recall it being a long week with a good bunch of guys, but you've got in the back of your mind that you are being assessed all the time. In the end you just have to crack on with it. They try to fatigue you – with lots of socialising and flying three times a day. After a few days you want to just chill out, but they push you to a point of such fatigue that you can't hide anything – your true personality comes out. Then you get the formal interview. So you are tired and working under pressure. That's exactly how it can get in the summer display season. Needless to say, I was absolutely speechless when I made it into the team!

The 2009 season marks my third and last with the team. Last year I was Red 5 and that position doubles as the 'Enid Uncle' – this means you've got to help mentor the new guys up front. The job of 'Exec' is another huge challenge as I am directly under the Boss as his number two and responsible for looking after his more mundane tasks, running the flying side of things and looking after the 'nitty gritty'. You actually end up being the grumpy one that cracks the whip a bit. If the Boss is ever raising his voice or getting upset, then I haven't done my job properly. If any problems start to occur I should nip them in the bud.

Public Display Authority

In order to put the final polish on the display, the Red Arrows swaps the sometimes unreliable weather of Lincolnshire for the guaranteed clear blue skies of RAF Akrotiri in Cyprus and the Springhawk detachment. The training season ends in May when the Commander-in-Chief, Air Command, makes an assessment of their safety and professionalism. If he is content, then he will award Public Display Authority, which is the team's formal authority to display in public. The nine display pilots are then allowed to wear their prestigious red flying suits for the first time. They are truly now Red Arrows, but with a hectic display season ahead of them, the hard work continues for pilots and support personnel alike.

Opposite above: The team briefs outside the operations block at RAF Akrotiri, Cyprus, during the Springhawk detachment (left). Flt Lt Mike Ling dons his flying kit at Scampton as he prepares for a Synchro training sortie (centre). Wg Cdr Jas Hawker checks in with the engineers as he prepares to 'walk' for a winter training sortie (right).

Opposite below: The team debriefs a display as standards officer Wg Cdr David Firth-Wigglesworth (left) known as Wing Commander RAFAT, listens in.

Following pages left: Over the top of a loop. With Scampton below, the Boss leads the formation into a loop through a break in the clouds. The team can switch to a full display from a flat show if the weather improves, and vice versa.

Following pages right: The team pilots wait expectantly for visitors to join them for one of the many photo sessions that are part of the routine each day, at the end of flying activities.

Above: Synchro – low down. The work up for the Synchro Pair involves flying dynamic manoeuvres down to 100ft. This is often over the sea and requires an incredible amount of training, judgement and skill.

Opposite: Smiles all round as Wg Cdr Jas Hawker, Sqn Ldr Ben Murphy, Flt Lt Damo Ellacott and Flt Lt Greg Perilleux walk back to the locker room after a successful practice display at Akrotiri.

| RED ARROWS

CREW

'Holding the Bank'

The support team

When you are dealing with 30-year-old aircraft and you need nine of them in the air, sometimes four times a day, you need a very special team of engineers to keep them serviceable. The Reds place huge emphasis on the support team that works tirelessly, day in, day out, to keep the team's Hawk T1s in the air. It's a big job.

The team's 85 engineering technicians and engineering support staff are headed by a three-strong senior management team, the Senior Engineering Officer or SEngO, the Junior Engineering Officer (JEngO) and a Flight Sergeant. It is this team that is directly responsible for ensuring that the right number of Hawks are available for the pilots during both the display and training seasons, and that the aircraft undergo the appropriate servicing and maintenance.

Squadron Leader Garry Ball joined the Reds as SEngO in 2008 and he works alongside JEngO Flt Lt Charlotte Fenn and senior 'engineering' Blue Flight Sergeant Steve Cox.

Flt Lt Charlotte Fenn

" My job is divided into two clear parts. In the summer I am responsible for the delivery of nine jets for the display and as part of that I also fly with the Boss as 'Circus 1' – so that means I take on usual 'Liney' duties which involve working down the line checking the aircraft before the next flight. The rest of the time I look after the 85 engineers, suppliers, photographers, drivers, survival equipment fitters (squippers) – all the support aspects. Circus is selected from the 85 Blues and we have a cross-section of engineering trades that we take on the road with the team. "

Sgt Paul Brown

" Nine aircraft engineering technicians are chosen each year to form Circus. These engineers are each allocated to a specific pilot for the duration of the summer display season. They fly in the back seat of the Hawk to and from display airfields and service the aircraft before and after

every display. The unique experience of flying regularly in a fast jet means that these are some of the most sought-after engineering jobs in the RAF. I was selected to be Circus leader in 2009. I only joined the squadron in 2008 and getting the Circus leader slot came as a welcome surprise.

I previously worked on the engineering wing at RAF Waddington and before that on the search and rescue force at Leconfield. I have an avionics background and when I joined the Reds I had to go back to RAF Cosford for my multi-skilled training as an electrician. I've had to get my line training as well as a Cat 1 medical for the Hawk passenger flying. I had never flown in a fast jet before and now all display season I will be flying with Red 9.

My role as leader of Circus involves co-ordinating all the groundcrews, the rectifications team (rects) and helping make sure there are nine aircraft ready to display. We can undertake some maintenance work on the line but we usually report it to Sgt Chris Marks in Rects Control who then sends out relevant personnel to fix the snag. If it's something simple like a bulb out, then aircrew accept it and we fix it at the end of the day. Members of Circus are all avionics, mechanical and armourers, we need at least one of each trade. Avionics guys deal with the electronics of the aircraft, mechanical engineers look after structure and the moving parts, while the armourers look after weapons on a combat squadron – at the Reds it is more geared towards the Hawk's ejection seats for them. There are five Circus reserves, they will cover illness and absences. Once we complete PDA (Public Display Authority) we get our blue suits and it's non-stop then right through to October. "

Above: The Blues – a fine shot of the 85-strong support team. Without these hard-working professionals, the Red Arrows would simply not function.

Opposite: A perfect Diamond Nine, one of the team's impressive signature formations.

Previous pages left: Senior Aircraftsman (SAC) Dan Conway tends to 'his' jet after arrival at an airshow. Every year a number of engineers from the Blues are selected to form Circus and transit throughout the season with a specific pilot to support his jet on the road.

Previous pages right: Engines running, the 'Lineys' prepare to 'see off' the Boss' jet during winter training (left). Arguably one of the nerve centres of the squadron – the Line and Engineering Control office (centre). SAC Roberts marshals Flt Lt Dave Davies back to his parking slot during winter training (right).

Above: Sgt Mark 'Flash' Jones and Cpl Mark 'Ted' Heath go through the formal paperwork for the jets as the pilots finish their pre-show briefing.

Opposite above: Flt Sgt Andy Bedford mans his desk at Rectification Control, ordering spares, co-ordinating maintenance work and generally running the engineering show (left). SAC Gaz Lewis talks over a small 'snag' with one of the jets as the pilots huddle around Red 5's wing after returning from a few days on the road (centre). Cpl Phil Ackerley performs post-flight cockpit checks on the Hawk after arriving at a show (right).

Opposite below: With flight kit left on the wing after arrival at the next show venue, Circus swings into action, checking oil levels, inspecting the jets and refuelling ready for the show.

"... the aircraft are dismantled,
inspected and tested to make sure that
any hidden faults are rectified ..."

Above: *Cpl Pete Targett checks the pressurisation of the wing fuel tanks of one of the team's Hawks during deep winter maintenance.*

Right: *Cpl 'Alfie' Heaton fits a new intake fairing to one of the Hawks in the hangar at Scampton during maintenance to repair a bird strike. The black intake has been drawn from another RAF Hawk, which was painted gloss black.*

Preparing the aircraft

Winter training is hard work for the whole squadron, with the team's fleet of 13 Hawk T1s given a thorough overhaul by the engineers. For each aircraft this takes between four and 16 weeks to complete. The aircraft are dismantled, inspected and tested to make sure that any hidden faults are rectified. This work must run to a tight schedule so that winter pilot training is not disrupted and the aircraft are prepared in time for the summer display season. Preparation of the aircraft begins each day at 06.30, when the first technicians arrive. A night shift works into the early hours of the morning to make sure that there are sufficient aircraft to carry out the following day's flying schedule.

In the summer season, if the team is carrying out a single display at one venue on one day, support is limited to the engineers who fly in the back of each aircraft (only during transits and not during displays). Red Arrows admin and logistics staff will have already made arrangements with the host airfield for aircraft parking and refuelling facilities. According to long-serving team Warrant Officer

John May, the team's Adjutant until 2008: 'If the team is directed to carry out more than one display on a given day, we will pre-position an enhanced team of engineers at the operating airfield. This small team will include five engineers whose primary task is to replenish the diesel/dye tank which generates the red, white and blue smoke so familiar to air display audiences across the world. If an overnight stay is required, support staff will also have made arrangements for accommodation and transport for pilots and engineers as well as proper security for our aircraft.'

Above: SAC Liam O'Keeffe notes down the hours from the aircraft's fatigue counter following a few days on the road. The 'life' of these Hawks has to be carefully managed by the team.

Right: Sgt Carl Roberts drafts in support from the road team to fix a problem with one of the team jets. For major shows on the UK mainland, a support engineering team travels by coach to each venue to supplement Circus.

SAC Rob Wheeler

"I am an avionics technician by trade. The electrical systems in the Hawk are very similar to other types and it is possible to take your experiences from other aircraft as you move around jobs in the RAF. Here I currently work on the aircraft rectification (Rects) team and this is an excellent place to be. Wherever you go in the RAF, everyone is just so busy all year round.

Currently I am working on a throttle top. I took the throttle control out of one of the jets this morning because one of the pilots reported a recurring problem. On top of the throttle you have the airbrake control for the Hawk. This is vital for the pilots as they use the airbrake all the time during the display. So I am fitting a brand new throttle top and re-wiring it all. My Sergeant is in charge of the job and allocated me to the actual repair, fitting brand new parts from stores. If the Circus guys out on the line encounter a major problem like this that can't be fixed in situ, they pass it to us to repair.

The opportunity to be selected for Circus is something most of us aspire to in our five-year tour on the team. It is great to be a part of the Red Arrows. I have done two tours in Afghanistan on the Chinook and it was great to come to Scampton to do something different. This is a totally different challenge but the rewards are just the same – it's all about keeping aircraft in the air."

Above: In the heat of the day during Springhawk training in Cyprus, the engineers swarm over the jets between practice displays, in readiness for the next launch.

Opposite: Jacked up forlornly at Scampton, the winter period allows for deep maintenance of the team's Hawks, ready for the push to Cyprus and ensuing display season.

"... the opportunity to be selected for Circus is something most of us aspire to ..."

SAC Stu Chapman

"I joined the RAF in 1998 and did my basic training at Halton before engineering training at Cosford. The Reds is a five-year tour for engineers and 2009 is my third season. Everyone wants Circus when they come here. I started off working on rectifications and I'm an avionics technician by trade. I then joined the dye team and went on Eastern Arrow to Malaysia. Then I got selected for the Circus 2 slot, so I flew all of 2008 with Red 2 Flt Lt Simon 'Kermit' Rea. Part of this included the Canada and America tour. It was an awesome tour. We transited through Greenland and I remember taking off and seeing huge icebergs in the water off the end of the runway.

In the season, my working day starts with a before flight (BF) check on the jet. I check the oil and do some general servicing. We then tow the aircraft out to the line; I sit in the cockpit and 'ride the brakes'. We can take our travel kit in the Hawk's pannier, which straps into a panel under the fuselage. In my jet we take the bags for Red 2 and 5 as Red 5's jet has a special wheel change pannier. Everyone is responsible for different bits of kit to take.

Above right: SAC Stu Roberts does the rounds with a cleaning cloth to ensure all bugs are removed from the windscreens. A dirty canopy can be very distracting for a Reds' pilot.

Right: SAC Gaz Lewis performs the pre-flight walkround check for his assigned jet in preparation for the arrival of the pilot. The groundcrews thoroughly check the aircraft, enabling the pilots to climb straight in.

I look after the oxygen kit. So, half an hour before we are due to take off, I do the walkround check, take out the engine intake blanks, turn on the oxygen in the jet and then strap in ready for the pilots to come out.

The transit is the easy bit, and once we land I get straight on with turnaround servicing, checking oil reservoir levels, tyres, looking for any leaks, checking down the intake for chips in the blades, clean the canopy, safe the back seat ready for the pilots to go and fly their display. We don't fly in the display.

When the aircraft are ready to taxi out we do what we call a 'see off'. We have a formal and informal version of this; the former is done when we have a crowd watching us. For this, all our actions are timed off the man in the middle at Red 5's jet. ”

Left: SAC Dan Conway removes the refuelling hose after filling up the Hawk. The Red Arrows have their own drivers who operate the team's 20 vehicles – everything from a 38-ton articulated tractor to fuel bowsers..

Following pages left: Phil Ackerley helps 'Boomer' strap in for a Springhawk sortie in Cyprus.

Following pages right: As soon as the engine has spooled down and the pilot has climbed out, the engineers set to work. As fuel arrives, the dye team's truck is already working its way down the line, with engineers working in the cockpit.

Above and right: *The Red Arrows' engineering support team comprises transport drivers, suppliers, photographers and survival equipment fitters (squippers). Cpl Dave Wright attends to one of the pilot's Mk10 helmets.*

Above: *Spare tyres – the team manages a vast supply of spare parts that are necessary to keep the Hawks in the air.*

Right: *Survival equipment fitter Cpl Mick Nicholson on the road with the team works on a loose connection affecting one of the pilot's oxygen masks.*

Engineering trades

Avionics engineers are responsible for all electrical and avionic systems on the Hawk. The equipment that they maintain ranges from simple emergency compasses to complex engine control circuits. They are also responsible for minor upgrades to the aircraft, such as a new engine performance monitoring system, which enables the condition of each engine to be managed more efficiently.

The Red Arrows have a 30-strong mechanical team specialising in two main areas: aircraft structure and the propulsion system. The aircraft structure includes not only the airframe but also the hydraulic undercarriage and flying controls and the cockpit environmental control system. In addition to the Rolls Royce Adour jet engine, they also maintain the aircraft fuel system and gas turbine starter.

The smallest of the three aircraft engineering trades, the seven-strong weapons team, is responsible for the maintenance and control of all explosive components and survival equipment fitted to the Hawk aircraft. This includes the Martin Baker Mk10B ejection seats, electrically initiated engine fire suppression system and emergency flying and landing gear systems. Collectively known as 'armourers', their jobs range from replacing emergency oxygen cylinders to aircraft ejection seats.

The Red Arrows' engineering support team comprises transport drivers, suppliers, photographers and survival equipment fitters (squippers). With a fleet of over 20 vehicles, the Red Arrows also have their own drivers who operate everything from refuelling bowsers to a 38-ton articulated tractor and trailer. When the team is operating away from Scampton, the support team also ensures that equipment and personnel are delivered on time to display venues.

The team's two photographers have a vital job of videoing every display from the ground, footage which is then swiftly delivered to the pilots for debriefing each practice of a public display. This is a key tool in perfecting the polished display, with the team able to analyse each element of the display in minute detail. The photographers are also responsible for much of the team's stunning stills photography.

The three squippers maintain all elements of the pilots' safety equipment, from helmet, oxygen mask and anti-G trousers to parachute and liferaft.

Above and above left: Sgt Ian Lindsay, Sgt Paul Brown and Cpl Tim Elton work on the Form 700 official logbooks for each of the team's Hawk aircraft. These are used to record faults, fixes and other data relating to each aircraft.

"... favourite
manoeuvres simply
wouldn't be possible
without the smoke
... a smoke plot is
worked out extremely
carefully to ensure that
no aircraft runs out of
smoke before the end
of the display ..."

The dye team

The famous phrase 'Smoke on GO!' is made possible by
the dye team. They are the guys in the silver suits who
swing into action after every display to replenish the diesel
and dye used to create the famous smoke trails. These are
actually vapour trails and are critical to flight safety as well
as enhancing the impact of the display. The smoke helps
Red 1 to judge wind speed and direction, and allows the
aircraft to locate each other in the second half of the show
when different sections of aircraft are frequently several
miles apart. Favourite manoeuvres such as the Heart simply
wouldn't be possible without the smoke.

The white smoke is produced by injecting diesel into
the hot exhaust from the jet engine, where it vaporises
immediately. The blue and red colours are made by mixing
dye with the diesel. The two consituents are stored in a
specially modified pod fitted under each aircraft. The pilot
releases the liquid by pushing one of three buttons on the
control column in the cockpit. He has seven minutes-worth
of smoke, five minutes of white and one minute each of red
and blue smoke. For this reason, a 'smoke plot' is worked
out extremely carefully to ensure that no aircraft runs out of
smoke before the end of the display.

Filling the tanks

Replenishing the diesel/dye mixture is a messy business and
is carried out in two separate operations. The dye rig truck
contains the red and blue dye/diesel mixture and this is fed
into the pod via a valve at the front. With no gauges on the
pod it is difficult to tell when the pod is full, but to avoid
overfilling and venting of the dye mixture, one member of
the team has to press an ear up against the back of the pod
to hear when the valve begins to quietly 'chatter' – time to
quickly close the valve!

Above: The white, blue and red smoke is made by mixing dye with diesel. The dye and diesel are stored in a specially modified pod fitted under each aircraft.

Above right: The dye team swings into action after every display to replenish the diesel and dye used to create the famous smoke trails.

Opposite: Decked out in their protective suits, the dye team swelter on the flightline at Cyprus as they head out to meet the team's Hawks as they return from another practice session.

Right: Pre-flight preparations: Red 1 runs through checks to make sure all the control surfaces are working correctly.

HAWK

'Roll, Go!'

The Hawk aircraft

The BAE Systems Hawk T1 two-seat jet trainer has been flown by the Red Arrows since the team took delivery of its first examples in the autumn of 1979. The Hawk is still used by the team today which is a testament to the quality, strength and durability of this incredible aircraft. Indeed, the team intends to keep flying the type until around 2018 on current estimates. With the Hawk, the Red Arrows have staged displays around the globe, from Europe to the USA and Canada, the Middle and Far East, Africa, Russia and Australia.

The first Hawker Siddeley P1182 Hawk flew back on 21 August 1974, and the type has since gone from strength to strength as it has evolved to offer jet training in support of frontline fighter aircraft types. With design work having been transferred from Kingston to Brough in 1988, followed by final assembly and flight test moving from Dunsfold to Warton in 1989 – it has been a story of constant evolution for the type, and for the original manufacturer, which has evolved from being British Aerospace into BAE

Systems. British Aerospace also produces a single-seat Hawk 200 fighter version. The Hawk is still in production at Brough and over 900 aircraft have been supplied to 19 customers around the world. Most recent customers include Australia, Canada, South Africa, Bahrain and India.

Hawk into service

The RAF ordered 176 Hawk T1s to replace the Folland Gnat and today it still operates the same aircraft for advanced flying and weapon training, with the Service ceremonially flying its one millionth Hawk flight hour on 5 July 2006. On successful completion of the Basic Fast Jet Training course on the Tucano, young pilots who have made the grade for advanced fast jet training move to RAF Valley to begin flying the Hawk with No 4 FTS. At Valley, new pilots join Nos 208(R) and 19(R) Squadrons for fast jet and advanced weapons training on the Hawk.

The Hawk is also used by Central Flying School to train instructors and by No 100 Squadron at RAF Leeming

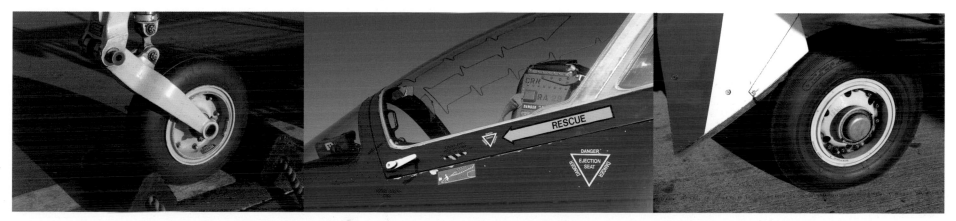

Previous pages left: A pair of Red Arrows BAE Systems Hawks power along at low level over the sparkling clear waters around the coast of Cyprus.

Previous pages right: Hawk in detail. The nose wheel, with chocks in place (left). The Hawk features a one-piece canopy that hinges to the right. A Miniature Detonation Cord (MDC) would shatter the canopy in the event of an ejection (centre). The left main undercarriage wheel of the Hawk (right).

Following pages right: The classic lines of the graceful Hawk T1. The Hawk is a tough airframe and a delight to handle – perfect for the Red Arrows.

for 'aggressor' duties and fast jet Weapon Systems Officer (WSO) training. It is also used for Forward Air Controller training with the Joint Forward Air Control Training and Standards Unit.

Having seen development from the original Hawk T1 version to the Hawk 50 and 60 series for export between 1980 and 1997, the Hawk 100 is the current enhanced version. The original Hawk has been transformed from its original configuration to today's impressive Mk128 – Advanced Jet Trainer (AJT). One of the most significant changes with the Hawk 100 was the development of its capabilities as a lead-in fighter trainer (LIFT). This featured a new 'combat wing', Adour Mk 871 or Mk 951 engine, new night vision goggles-compatible 'glass cockpit', MIL-STD-1553B digital databus, new head-up display and hands-on throttle and stick controls.

The RAF's new Hawk version is the Mk128, with 28 new aircraft on order. This enhanced version will dramatically upgrade the RAF's training output in terms of allowing students to emerge from training with an enhanced understanding of modern systems including advanced digital cockpits. The biggest development for the latest Hawk is embedded simulation with capabilities such as radar training through the exchange of aircraft data via a datalink. This allows up to six aircraft to communicate with each other and will show on the display as a radar simulation as if it were real, without the expense of employing an actual radar. The mission support and planning system means that the instructor can set up simple intercepts with a pre-planned mission.

In the cockpit

Red Arrows pilots wear an array of survival equipment. This includes Alpha Mk10B helmet and oxygen mask, life-saving jacket (LSJ), anti-G trousers and leg restraints. The anti-G trousers feature bladders that inflate when the aircraft is pulling high G-forces. They envelop the legs and abdomen and help keep blood in the upper body. The leg restraints are part of the ejection system and help prevent the pilot's legs from flailing around in the event of an ejection. The aircraft features two Martin-Baker Mk10 ejection seats.

Right: Flt Lt Dave Davies shows off the flying kit worn by Red Arrows pilots. The life-saving jacket (LSJ) features survival equipment including a locator beacon plus flotation gear. The G-pants zip up over the flying suit like a horse-rider's chaps. These feature inflatable bladders that squeeze the abdomen and legs at high G-force levels to help to keep the blood in the upper body and so prevent blackout. Just below the knee are the leg restraint garters. These clip on and once in the cockpit, the pilot threads leg restraint lanyards through two loops on the front of the garters to restrict leg flail in the event of an ejection.

Opposite: The Mk10B helmet is standard throughout the RAF and with the Reds. The helmet features clear and dark visors, important protection in the event of ejection or bird strike. The oxygen mask is attached by two 'chains' and also features a communications microphone.

Above: The complex cockpit of the 1970s vintage Hawk T1. The aircraft does not feature any clever computers, or modern digital displays; it's all analogue displays and pilot skill that makes this aircraft tick. In the centre at the top of the console is one piece of new 'kit' – a GPS with map. The pan of the ejection seat is also seen in this shot, with the round black and yellow QRF (Quick Release Fitting) lying on the cushion. The QRF is the main fitting into which all seat straps are secured. The front can be twisted for a quick release of all straps.

Left: As he unstraps, Sqn Ldr Graham Duff inserts his shoulder straps into the stowage lugs on the headreast of the Martin-Baker ejection seat.

Opposite: The green leg restraint lanyards can be seen draped over knobs on the main pilot instrument panel. The artificial horizon sits centrally with other primary flight instruments around it, including altimeter, speed and heading indicators.

"... on successful completion of the Basic Fast Jet Training course on the Tucano, young pilots who have made the grade for advanced fast jet training move to RAF Valley to begin flying the Hawk with No4 FTS ..."

Previous pages left: *The explosive Miniature Detonating Cord (MDC) is clearly seen in this silhouette photograph of the Hawk canopy. When closing the canopy, the pilot lowers his visor and closes his eyes for protection in the event of an accidental triggering of the MDC system.*

Previous pages right: *Sunlight streams through the join of the small trim tab on the rudder. This allows the pilot to fine-tune his controls and correct small control errors.*

Above: *Deep maintenance is carried out in the main hangar at Scampton. The team's Hawks are lifed to 8000 flight hours and the rigours of flying with the team mean that the engineers have to work hard to keep the aircraft in mint condition.*

Opposite: *The hot end of the Hawk. The exhaust of the Rolls-Royce Adour engine features three pipes that are unique to the team's aircraft. These pump the diesel and dye into the hot exhaust gases to produce the famous 'smoke' trails.*

"... the Hawk is still used by the team today which is a testament to the quality, strength and durability of this incredible aircraft ..."

The Hawk

The Hawker Siddeley Hawk first flew on 21 August 1974, signalling the start of the first-generation of Hawk trainers. The life of the RAF Hawk structure has been extended from 6,000 to 12,500 flight hours, with the fatigue index raised from 100 to 150FI.

The diagrams here depict a Hawk T1. This example carries the under fuselage Aden gun pack, which is replaced by a special pod for the diesel/dye mix for the smoke trails when the aircraft is flown by the Red Arrows.

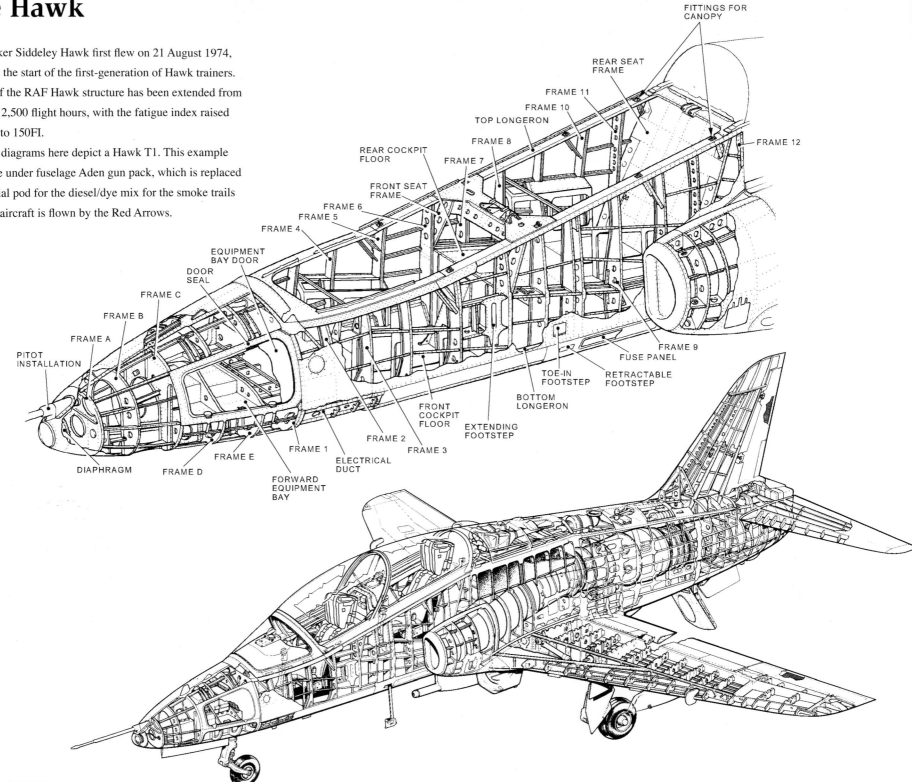

BAE SYSTEMS

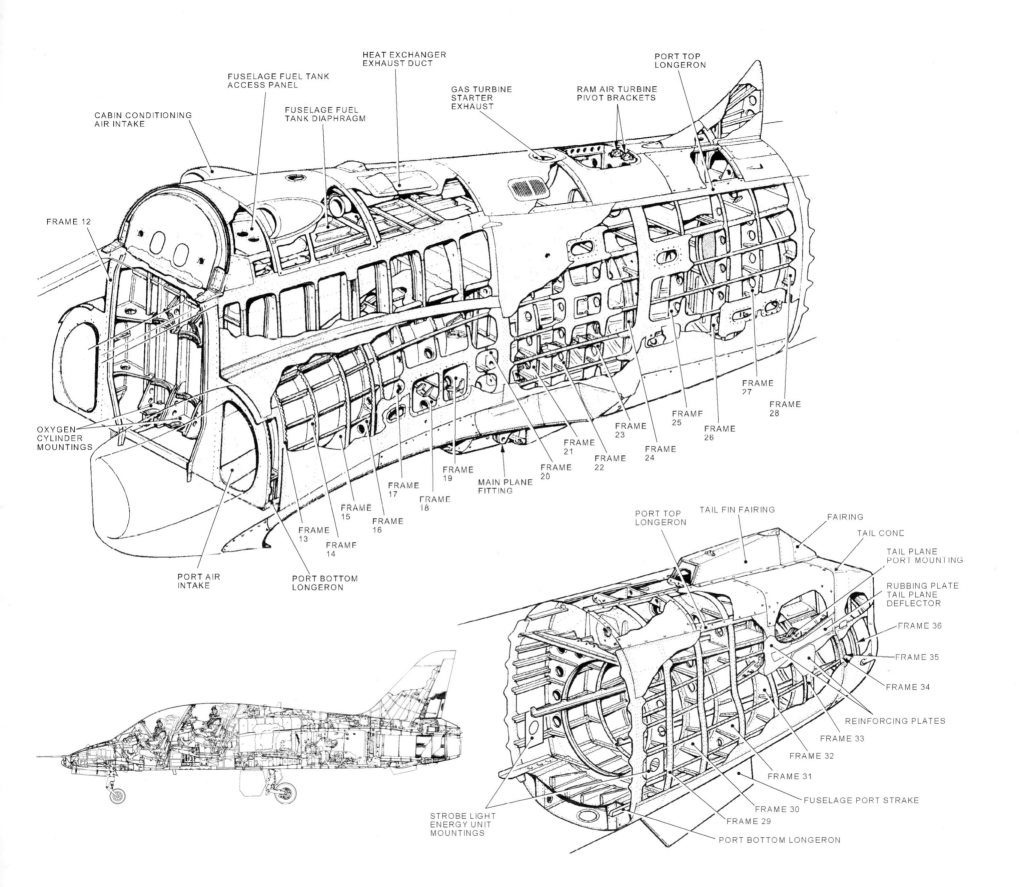

CABIN CONDITIONING
AIR INTAKE

FRAME 12

OXYGEN
CYLINDER
MOUNTINGS

FUSELAGE FUEL TANK
ACCESS PANEL

FUSELAGE FUEL
TANK DIAPHRAGM

HEAT EXCHANGER
EXHAUST DUCT

GAS TURBINE
STARTER
EXHAUST

PORT TOP
LONGERON

RAM AIR TURBINE
PIVOT BRACKETS

GAS TURBINE
STARTER
EXHAUST

FRAME
27

FRAME
28

FRAME
25

FRAME
26

FRAME
23

FRAME
24

FRAME
21

FRAME
22

FRAME
19

FRAME
20

FRAME
18

FRAME
17

MAIN PLANE
FITTING

FRAME
15

FRAME
16

FRAME
13

FRAME
14

PORT AIR
INTAKE

PORT BOTTOM
LONGERON

PORT TOP
LONGERON

TAIL FIN FAIRING

FAIRING

TAIL CONE

TAIL PLANE
PORT MOUNTING

RUBBING PLATE
TAIL PLANE
DEFLECTOR

FRAME 36

FRAME 35

FRAME 34

REINFORCING PLATES

FRAME 33

FRAME 32

FRAME 31

FUSELAGE PORT STRAKE

FRAME 30

FRAME 29

PORT BOTTOM LONGERON

STROBE LIGHT
ENERGY UNIT
MOUNTINGS

Powering the Hawk

Adour engine in detail

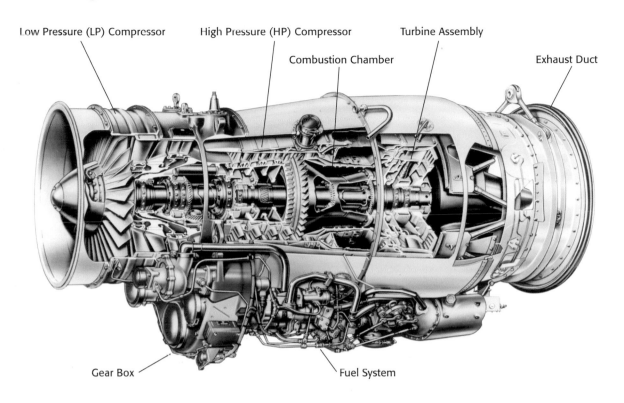

Low Pressure (LP) Compressor High Pressure (HP) Compressor Turbine Assembly

Combustion Chamber Exhaust Duct

Gear Box Fuel System

Rolls Royce Adour

The Red Arrows' Hawks are powered by a single 5240lb thrust Adour Mk151-02 non-afterburning turbofan. The Adour Mk151 coupled with the Hawk has remained one of the most potent trainer/light combat aircraft systems available. With the advent of its latest and most advanced variant, the Mk951, the Adour engine has continued a process of evolution which has seen it benefit from the integration of the very latest in both civil and defence engine technologies.

Developed by the joint venture company Rolls-Royce Turbomeca, the Adour engine first entered service in 1972 with the Jaguar fleets of the Royal Air Force and France's L'Armée de l'Air. Generating between 7305lbf and 8400lbf thrust with afterburner, those reheated engines went on to power Jaguars for Ecuador, Oman, India and Nigeria, as well as the indigenous T2 and F1 aircraft in Japan. In 1980, Finland was the first customer for the export version of the Hawk, the Mk50, powered by the Adour Mk851. The 6000lb

thrust Adour Mk871 is the current engine for the Hawk 100 trainer. Rolls-Royce is incorporating technologies from the Mk871 engine into a new variant, the Adour Mk821, which is being offered to India for its Jaguar upgrade requirement.

Continued improvements

The latest Adour, the Mk951, was launched in response to customer requirements and features improved performance of eight per cent of thrust relative to the Mk871, with up to twice the target time between overhaul. The Mk951 also has a FADEC (Full Authority Digital Electronic Control) system which provides engine-handling assistance for pilots and is available for all current variants of the Hawk family. Deliveries of the Adour Mk951 began to launch customer South Africa in 2005 and the engine has also been ordered by Bahrain and the UK. Over 2800 Adours have been delivered to date, clocking up over seven-and-a-half million flying hours.

Above: The new Adour Mk951 features a FADEC (Full Authority Digital Electronic Control) which reduces pilot workload.

Above right: The Adour is a two-shaft engine, with a two-stage fan and five-stage High Pressure Compressor.

SHOW

'Letting It Out'

Behind the scenes

The sun beats down on a dusty roadway, the blue sky contrasts starkly with the yellow rocks. It's hot, but a sea breeze keeps the temperature comfortable. In the distance a radio crackles, 'Reds … prime'. Suddenly a distant rumble turns into a rush of air and a whistle of jets – nine Hawks sweep majestically over the cliffs and out to sea – 'annnnd … pulling up!' It's important for the Reds to have an uninterrupted period of training to hone the finer points of the display. So in late March the team departs en masse to RAF Akrotiri in Cyprus for Exercise Springhawk – a welcome chance to make use of the beautiful weather and put the finishing touches to the display during two intense months of flying in the Mediterranean. The RAF had some great overseas bases, Tengah in Singapore, Kai Tak in Hong Kong and Luqa in Malta, to mention a few. Akrotiri is the last of a dying breed of such bases. It's synonymous with fine weather, hard work and a great social scene.

The team briefs the three daily sorties outside the operations block on the dispersal, they work up a real sweat in the cockpit sun traps, the engineers work hard keeping the jets in tip-top condition, the administrators shuttle to and fro in air-conditioned four-wheel-drive Land Rovers – most agree it sure beats a dull and damp Lincolnshire.

Getting 'behind the scenes' of the Red Arrows gives an amazing insight into the daily life of this incredible team. One member of the team who interacts with the public more than any other is Red 10. For three years until the end of 2008, this vital role was fulfilled by the charismatic Flt Lt Andy Robins.

Flt Lt Andy Robins: Red 10

" The Red 10 job turned out to be nothing like I expected. The connotation is that you're just the Boss' bag carrier, but actually it's nothing like that – the variety is amazing. I need to be a Hawk pilot that is up to the high standards of the Reds, I have to play a big part in planning, plus I have the commentary. So there's lots of office time and pilot time – I have always referred to

myself as 'Oddjob'. One of my flying jobs is to act as photo chase for stills imagery and filming of the team in the air. I have learned so much about chasing the main formation, sun position for photos and trying to give a stable photo platform for the back-seat photographer. I have to keep out of the way of the team as they fly their display but get close enough for photos – it's quite challenging.

Ready for the season

In the winter period I am already planning ahead for the summer, I have the Cyprus detachment to arrange, UK displays to plan and perhaps something really long term like a tour where you are planning nine-12 months ahead. I was heavily involved in planning for the 2008 North American tour. It was amazing that we got clearance to display in New York, which I consider my crowning glory during my time with the team.

We flew just outside New York harbour – the closest any team has been allowed to display to the city. The boys displayed under the flightpath of three major airports,

Newark, La Guardia and JFK. It was a full rolling display and I remember an MD-11 airliner actually flew over the top at 3000ft as they completed the first half of the show. We managed to keep it all totally safe and brought off a real spectacle. During that tour I also loved doing the commentary at Quebec Airshow in French. I had to brush up a bit but it worked out really well.

In reality, the commentary only accounts for 5-10 per cent of my job. I am actually far busier planning, setting things up, checking new display sites that I have to survey and things like that. It's been great to take the team to new audiences, such as the music festival Global Gathering. We cold-called them as part of a plan to get the RAF in front of a new audience. A lot of people don't know who we are or what we do.

Crazy summer schedule

The summer season is totally run to the WHAM (what's happening manager?) and is totally reactive. In the summer a typical day will start with me flying a transit sortie out to

a display venue as the tenth jet in the formation. On arrival I hop into a helicopter or car to the venue, do the commentary and monitor the airspace for safety or infringements. Then jump back in the wheels to the Hawk, get airborne with the boys to the next venue, maybe back into a car, check the weather, commentate again, back to the airport and fly back.

To be honest, my day is probably less intense than the boys' really sharp peak of display flying, but mine is a lot longer so I leave earlier, get back later, with no spare time in the day. I often have to look after hotels as well. The Adjutant back at Scampton actually books them but I sort out the bills and logistics once we're there. The road manager is basically a firefighter, there to sort out any issues that arise. I have thoroughly relished the job and am passing the reins to Sqn Ldr Graeme Bagnall for 2009.

Left: Reds 1-5 of 'Enid' perform the Python during the second half of the display at Bournemouth Air Festival, watched by a huge seafront audience.

Opposite: Flt Lt Andy Robins, Red 10, whips up the crowd with his commentary on the show. The team has actively sought to engage new audiences, displaying at concerts and festivals.

Previous pages left: In Big Battle formation, the nine Hawks sweep over the cliffs at RAF Akrotiri, Cyprus.

Previous pages right: The famous operations block at Akrotiri, festooned with squadron artwork, with the pilots briefing in the sunshine (left). Flt Lts Pablo O'Grady and Andrew 'Boomer' Keith go over a few points from the sortie as they head back to the debrief. Cyprus allows the final polish to the show, prior to Public Display Authorisation, the big test and the culmination of the training (centre). The display finale – the famous Vixen Break photographed from Red 10 during a photo chase sortie with the team (right).

Sqn Ldr Graham Duff:
A day in the life of Red 8

"My alarm clock has such a piercing tone – rudely awakening me at 07.00. In no time I'm down to the hotel's breakfast room having perfected the 'stuffing' technique of packing. Staying in a different hotel every night for six months tends to make you fairly efficient. Kermit is already tucking into breakfast with the Boss; they're discussing how nice it would be to retire here in Jersey. They are looking at a beautiful blue sky and admiring the stunning view to the beach. Red 10, Andy, has paid the room bills with his corporate credit card and wheels leave at 08.00 sharp. For each minute you are late we have 'pigz' (see glossary on page 136) to the value of £1. Andy gets chatting to the hotel manager and is 11 seconds late setting off in his hire car. £1 thank you very much!

The engineers left the hotel an hour before we did and are already busy servicing the jets ready for a 10am take off. I always look forward to seeing my Circus backseater, SAC Peter 'Lamby' Lamb and he fills me in on any problems with the jet. The navigation officer is already busy. For this leg it's Lingy and he is already on the phone trying to get RAF Leuchars to understand how we plan to arrive into the airshow and find out what our arrival time-slot is. The bags need to be loaded into the Hawk's panniers, Red 3's job. The weather needs to be checked, Red 4. The hire cars need returning, Red 5. The Boss and Red 6 (Synchro Lead) are discussing the finer points of the upcoming display at Leuchars. So at 10.03 we are off to Leuchars, leaving the lovely Jersey coastline and sunny weather behind.

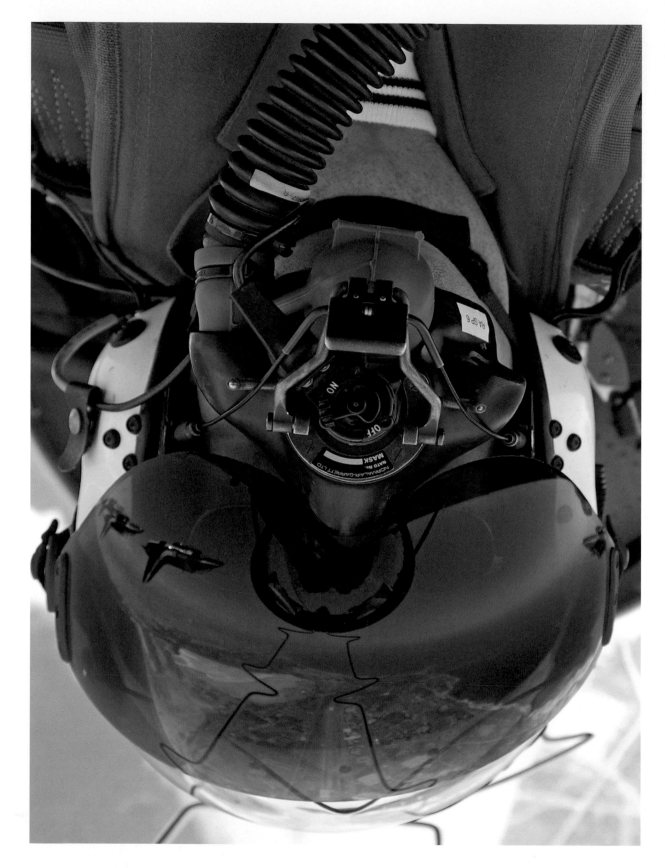

Above: Flt Lt Greg Perilleux dons his flying helmet as he gets ready for another display.

Right: Sweeping out of the blue, the azure sky is painted with white trails as the team puts on another polished show.

Opposite: Which way up? A good portion of a Red Arrows pilot's day is spent upside down!

Above: Smoke on GO! – running in for the arrival pass in Big Battle. Nine Hawks in perfect symmetry.

"... the show arrival always sends a shiver down my spine. Red 1 has got a tremendous voice over the radio and we all get pumped up by his commands as we run in over the crowd..."

Opposite: The team always tries to accommodate requests and tie displays and flypasts in with special events and occasions. Here, the team displays above HMS Illustrious *during a port visit to Limassol in Cyprus.*

Transits are largely uneventful and we fly in two sections of five jets, in close formation for the whole route. The Boss leads 'Enid' with Red 6 following in one-mile trail with 'Gypo'. It's hard work flying close formation for that long, but it is the only way to get 10-11 jets not to hit each other and fly in a strict one-mile box. Interestingly we fly in the same formation as flocks of migrating birds – it's just the easiest and most logical way to do it.

At 11.07 we arrive at a rather rainy and windy Leuchars and Lamby jumps out of the jet to put the chock under the nosewheel and get his Goretex jacket out of the nose bay. I let the brakes off and finish my checklist, switching off all the relevant systems in the Hawk. Red 4 left his flaps in the 'up' position as we parked – another £1! We all quickly meet at Red 5's wing to debrief any problems with the transit but quickly decide to do the chat in the waiting minibus as it's pouring down.

The display is in two hours time and Emma 'Trigger' Thomas, our pre-positioned public relations officer, has organised a signing session for us in the Red Arrows tent. A small queue has already formed and we set about signing brochures – it's been calculated that a Red Arrows pilot will sign his name over 10,000 times during the summer season. I love it – I'll sign anything.

We meet up again at 30 minutes to go to brief the show. We normally all lean on a wing and the Boss will go through any pertinent points from the last show, any obstacles for this show and then do a full run through of what he has planned. Red 6 then has a few minutes to brief everyone on the Synchro parts of the display – we are back

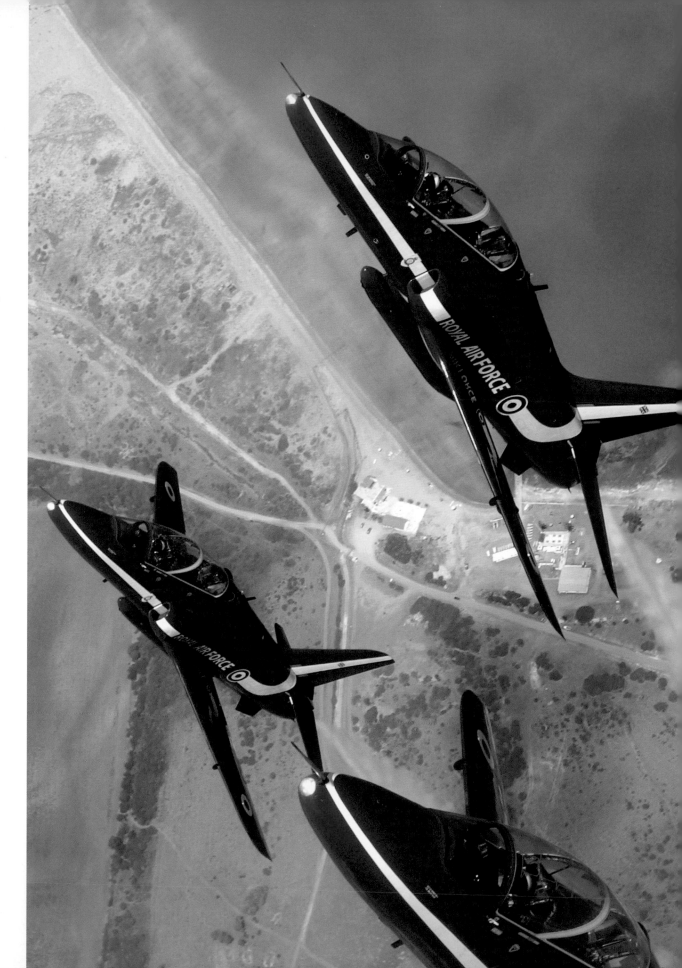

in the minibus as it's still raining. The Boss talks through a flat routine due to the low cloud plus it's going to be bumpy as it's windy. At the end of the brief Red 9, Boomer the Exec, adds some technique points for the new guys on how to avoid letting the bumps throw a pilot off position. After the Boss tells us the radio check in time, I walk down to my jet and strap in with the help of a very wet, but happy and smiling, Lamby. He is looking forward to us taxiing off, as that means he can grab a bite to eat and a warming coffee.

The show arrival always sends a shiver down my spine. Red 1 has got a tremendous voice over the radio and we all get pumped up by his commands as we run in over the crowd. Red 10 watches the show and as he commentates he calls us on the radio if he sees any safety or smoke problems. I got out of sync with my smoke during the Phoenix pass; I was switching it on when I should have been switching it off! Red 10 transmits '8 check smoke'. It causes me to glance at the smoke indicator…aargh! Another £1.

As we draw the show to a close, the air conditioning has dried the rain off my flying suit but I am now wet with sweat from the physicality of the show and sheer concentration. It's like doing the hardest crossword and playing squash, all while driving round a racetrack at full speed. Back on the ground we jump out and head for a video room to debrief the show video. The video is taken by our team photographer from the ground at crowd centre and we have to watch the video from the previous show before we display again. We watch the tape zoomed right in and pause every frame so we can scrutinise when the smoke is switched

Above: *Every display and practice is filmed by the team's photographic section. This allows the team to debrief in accurate detail and is pivotal in creating the perfect display.*

Left: *Joining up in formation over a beach in Cyprus shortly after take-off, viewed from Red 8.*

Opposite: *The team loops during a practice in Cyprus, with the windsurf club in the background. This beach provides some welcome relaxation for the team during Springhawk.*

on or off – we strive for total perfection so go into minuscule detail. My Phoenix error is paused in great Technicolor detail – much to the amusement of everyone else.

En route to France

The debrief takes half an hour, and we rush back to the jets to brief the transit to Roanne in France. I'm the Nav for this leg so I put on my best French accent to explain our procedures to the French controller on the telephone. All the weather is checked: it's nicer in France, blue sky awaits us and they have quite a crowd ready to welcome us. Lamby is pleased to be leaving Leuchars, but he soon steams up the canopy as he dries off. At 14.30 on the dot we depart for France. As the team crosses a time zone change on the map (also seen on the GPS), Red 10 has 10 seconds before or after to transmit 'Reds Timewarp' so everyone can change their watch. If he forgets, he gets pigz'd so it's customary to start a conversation with him with 30 seconds to go in the hope that he won't realise.

We land at Roanne at 16.45 due to the time shift and get ready for an evening display. Lovely blue skies and calm winds mean it's going to be a belter of a show. The French are very patriotic and prefer their team the 'Patrouille de France' so it's nice to wander through the crowd signing various posters and PR items after the display and see their positively surprised reaction to our show. Landing at 19.00 we save the video for tomorrow. We'll watch it before our next show in Norfolk. The engineers stay at the airport for as long as it takes to fix any jet snags and finish servicing their aeroplanes; in fact

we generally beat them to the hotel by an hour or two. The French hotel is a welcome sight and we meet in the foyer at 8.30 before looking for a restaurant. After eating too much and phoning home, I set my alarm for 7am. As I nod off I realise today the Red Arrows woke up in Jersey, displayed in Scotland, landed in France and wowed a French crowd with a full show in the evening.

Truly awesome – bring on tomorrow.'

"... blue sky awaits ... and they have quite a crowd ready to welcome us ..."

Opposite: *The team 'Spag Breaks' over Akrotiri during Springhawk. A typical Reds' day is a busy one – display flying, meeting the public, transit flying, hotels – and so is a complex time-keeping exercise.*

Left: *Synchro lead barrels in towards the display line during a show at RAF Shawbury.*

REDS' SPEAK

Pigz: A fining system adopted by the RAF to help increase punctuality and prevent errors. Basically each time you mess up you get 'pigz'd'. The Red Arrows Executive Officer keeps a tally of fines and the team has to pay their total every week into a fund. A 20p fine is levied for minor smoke crimes, such as switching your smoke on or off fractionally before everyone else. £5 for a major public mistake – wrong coloured smoke for a flypast, for example. In Cyprus a team member's bill could be as much as £50 a week! You learn quickly.

Full, Rolling and Flat: The three different display sequences, generally determined by cloud base or sometimes by airspace restrictions if performing near London, for example. The minimum cloud base for a Full display is 5000ft, for a Rolling display is 2500ft and a Flat display is 1000ft. The minimum visibility is 2 miles. Full is the preferred option as the team flies full looping manoeuvres, Rolling misses out the loops and includes rolls, and Flat takes the same time as the others but consists of a series of 'bends' in front of the crowd.

Navigation Officer: A second or third year pilot, not including the Boss, is nominated for each leg of a transit to each display. It is his job to organise the maps, route, liaison and fuel as well as dealing with the general planning involved. When airborne, Navigation Officers also do all the communication with air traffic, leaving the Boss free to concentrate on leading the formation.

RED ARROWS 9-SHIP FORMATIONS 2009

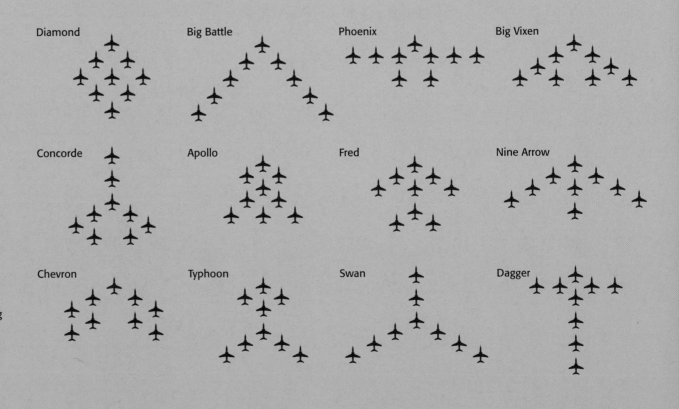

Diamond

Big Battle

Phoenix

Big Vixen

Concorde

Apollo

Fred

Nine Arrow

Chevron

Typhoon

Swan

Dagger

Above: The Reds arrive en masse at a summer airshow. The pilots are already debriefing and the Blues have swung into action.

Left: Sqn Ldr Graham Duff climbs aboard 'his' Hawk. Second or third year pilots are usually nominated to organise transits to and from displays. The role involves looking after the maps, route, liaison, fuel and general planning involved. In the transit this pilot then looks after communication with air traffic, allowing Red 1 to concentrate on leading the formation.

Previous pages left: The view from Red 10 as Flt Lt Andy Robins chases the formation into the Palm Tree and Synchro Split at the end of the first half of the 2008 show.

Previous pages right: Autumn sun catches one of the team's Hawks as they head back to Scampton after a long day 'on the road'.

Following pages left: The four 'Gypo' jets, Reds 6-9, power head on towards the crowd for the spectacular 'Gypo' break.

Following pages right: Red 6, 'Synchro Leader', piles on the G-forces as he turns in for an opposition crossover pass over the runway. Note the vortices streaming off the wingtips as the turn tightens.

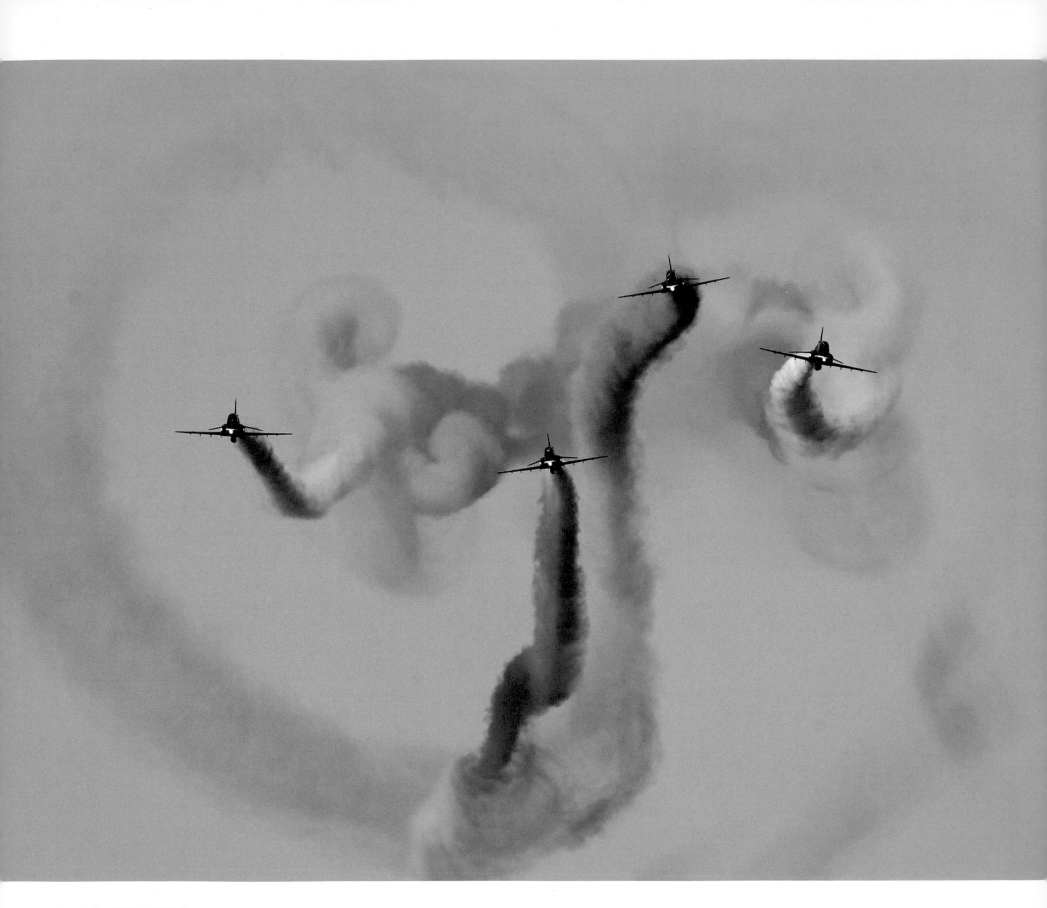

The administration team

There is just so much paperwork and organisation that is associated with the team. Squadron Leader Jon Trott is the team's non-aircrew manager and he heads the administration and flight planning teams that are responsible for the extensive planning and organisation behind the scenes. His role has also recently involved pivotal help in co-ordinating new official books about the team.

SAC Simon Miller

"I have been on the Red Arrows since October 2006 as part of the admin team. I work for Sqn Ldr Trott and the team Adjutant Warrant Officer Alan Murray and we look after everything from pay, to ringing embassies, looking after passport visas and things like that. We are also the first line of communication to the team with regard to external enquiries, and when the team is away one of us is always here manning the fort."

Cpl Pete Jones and Cpl Simon Evans

"We are responsible for flight operations planning. We take a lot of time forward planning for displays and events, we put out the NOTAMs (notices to airmen) and sort out diplomatic clearances for overseas trips. We generate the flying programme, notify the team of Royal Flights and generally keep the official documents up to date and help keep everything safe."

Public Relations

The Red Arrows have a busy and extensive programme of public relations activity – managed by a team of specialists including Nikki Wright and Emma Thomas. Public interest in the Red Arrows is intense and the small PR team handles hundreds of enquiries each week, as well as many visits by youth groups, VIPs and members of the public. The PR team also manages media enquiries, produces a wide range of promotional items, maintains the official website and organises the team's frequent public appearances.

'Gypo Going Full'

The display

Oh my goodness! We're 300 feet up, belting along at 500 miles per hour; the countryside is a green blur. A road, a car, a house, someone waving up at us – gone in a flash. Hard turn right, level off, take a breath, look for the Boss' smoke, hard turn left, 8G, crikey, an elephant has sat on my chest, don't grey out, don't grey out! I can feel the sweat making the oxygen mask slip down my face. How on earth does he know where the other guys are? 'Tum, te tum, te tum'. I smile to myself as my pilot takes it all in his stride. Ah, there's the Boss, my pilot saw him ages ago – I just caught up. We are closing fast. Airbrake out, straining against the seat straps, slide back into formation. I shake my head and chuckle to myself quietly – wow – how did you do that? In position, 'Reds, break, break, GO!' 'Roll, check a thousand, pull', aargh, more 8G.

Now try that for half an hour. That level of intensity, that level of concentration, milliseconds between life and death. It's that fine a line that a Red Arrows pilot walks. As a privileged passenger in the back seat, it is an awe-inspiring experience to witness at first hand a display. It is a total assault on the body and the senses. For the pilot it's a hard gym workout, it's the toughest memory game, it's pushing yourself to the absolute limit. There are no computers, there are no collision warning devices, there is no one to cover your behind – it's nine pilots, each using their eyes, their hands, their brains and their cockpit stopwatches to make this thing work.

The Red Arrows pilots make their flying machine do incredible things. It doesn't just take off, fly around a bit and get to its destination. It cavorts around the sky, feet away from eight other aircraft, low to the ground, upside down, smoke on, smoke off – shuddering with G-forces, howling with power – with a red-suited ace coaxing every last bit of performance out of this well-honed aeroplane. From the ground, it all seems so effortless, so graceful, and so perfect. Lazy arcs of white smoke punctuate the azure blue summer sky. Ooh, that was a close crossover, Wow, did you see that? What a show.

The pilots have a wonderfully relaxed air of confidence. They have total faith in each other's abilities and they trust each other implicitly. The picture in the formation is so very different from being on the ground watching as a spectator. From the ground the formation is immaculate, as one expects, as if the nine jets were joined as one. In the air it's a very different story. Small adjustments in formation to get the right line, formation changes, looping and rolling, all the while the gaggle of aircraft are hanging onto the leader's coat tails as if jostling for position – so close that they buffet and the coloured smoke stains their vertical fins.

A tale of two halves

The first half of the show ends with a big break, then the Boss leads 'Enid' through a series of different manoeuvres, the Vertical Break, Caterpillar, the famous Rollbacks to mention a few. Entwined with this 'Gypo' formation fly their routine including the Mirror Roll, Corkscrew and the Gypo Break. The timings are crucial. A stopwatch in the cockpit, beeps and calls on the radio, careful positioning and total situational awareness keep the two sections safely apart.

The part of the display that the crowd doesn't see is just as tough and can actually be more strenuous than the actual passes at crowd centre. Breaks mean rejoins are necessary, and during some portions of the second half of the display one or two jets from 'Gypo' have to flit across to join 'Enid'. Then race back to rejoin 'Gypo'. The show reaches its finale with the Gypo Break, a punishing 8G break of all four 'Gypo' jets – Reds 6-9. The Syncro Pair

then stays crowd centre for one last series of crossovers, meanwhile Reds 8 and 9 charge away unseen to join the Boss and 'Enid' for the last part of the spectacle – the Vixen Break.

Left: How close? The famous Synchro Pair perform incredible crossover manoeuvres at crowd centre. They are actually very close and the two pilots must have total trust in one another.

Previous pages left: Even in a vertical break like this, the Red Arrows are working on immaculate and very exact spacing to give the maximum visual effect.

Previous pages right: Head out of the cockpit, the pilots have to use total concentration, watching everything going on around them (left). The pilots not only have to concentrate on their timing, and team mates, but they also have to endure crushing G-forces (centre). The view from the back seat of Red 7 as the Synchro Pair perform a crossover split. The minimal spacing between the aircraft means that practice and timing is everything (right).

Following pages left: The team flies the Phoenix Bend. The spacing and positioning in this formation is very tricky and any minor errors are very evident.

Following pages right: The team comes over the top of a loop while practising in Cyprus. The beach below stretches away towards Limassol.

Above: 'Reds airborne'. The Boss calls air traffic control to alert them to the fact that the team is in the air and preparing to display. It is important that air traffic monitors the strict airspace regulations that the team requires. No other aircraft are permitted near the team when it is displaying on strict safety grounds.

Opposite: The view from Red 8 in the Phoenix Bend. On the outside of the formation, the Red 8 slot requires a lot of movement in the rolling manoeuvres as the aircraft has much further to revolve around the leader than the aircraft close to him, such as Reds 2 and 3. This is why positions such as Reds 8 and 9 tend to be filled by second or third year pilots.

"... the pilots have a wonderfully relaxed air of confidence. They have total faith in each other's abilities and they trust each other implicitly ..."

Left: *Following the Goose, Reds 1-5 'Enid' (seen here) trail coloured smoke and enter the Steep Climb.*

.

Opposite: *The Goose. Red 8 pulls up hard into an 8G climb having passed through 'Enid' formation. This is a good example of how 'Gypo' aircraft have to flit between the two sections in the second half of the show. After this manoeuvre, Red 8 has to power round to rejoin 'Enid' for the seven aircraft Vertical Break. He then rejoins 'Gypo' for the Corkscrew.*

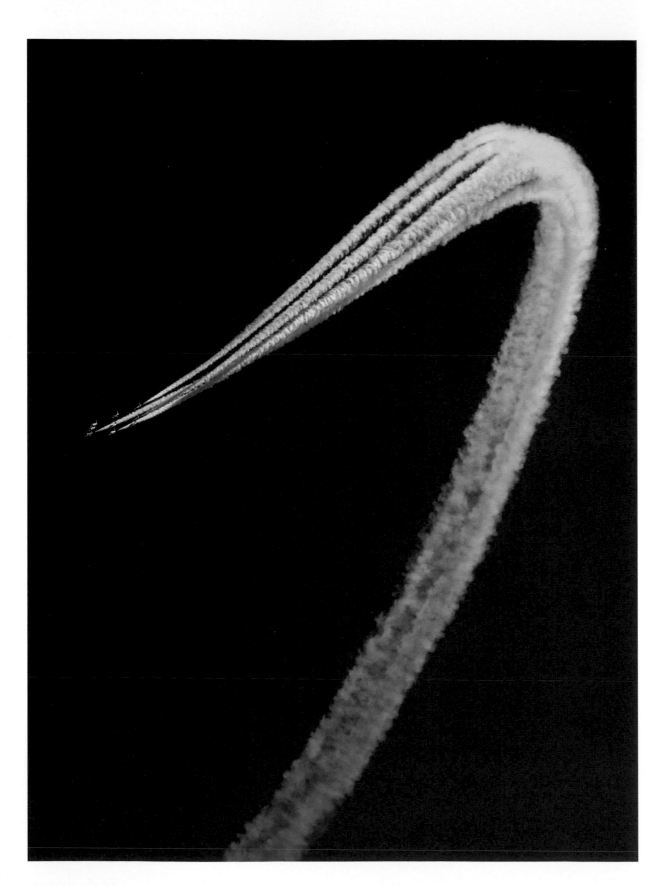

Sqn Ldr Graham Duff: The view from Red 8

For the 2009 display I have moved out to Red 8, which is normally the jet farthest out on the right-hand side. It is a great privilege to fly in this slot as I am the right-hand side's coach for the display's first half and I get to do to some awesome 'Gypo' manoeuvres in the second half. Red 9, the farthest left, and myself have the best vantage point to assess each pilot's handling skills during the flight, as we look 'through' them to the leader and are able to offer advice, tips and criticism when required. We have a very honest and open culture during our debriefs; pride does not feature, which is good, as it could get very dented! This time Red 4 seems to be moving the control column too much as he reacts to Red 2's movements, whereas Red 2 is occasionally sitting too 'long', so needs to move forward a bit, or is 'shallow' so he needs to move up a bit.

The Corkscrew manoeuvre in the display involves Reds 6 and 7 flying level upside down along the length of the crowd with me about three aeroplane lengths behind barrel rolling round their smoke and 9 doing barrel rolls in the opposite direction three aeroplane lengths behind me. We do three complete barrel rolls before rolling out. The view out of the cockpit as you roll round the front jets is phenomenal. Red 6 shouts '8 and 9 roll GO!' and we both set off. The difficulty is maintaining the three lengths behind the aircraft in front. Getting 'short' is alarming for me as I get close to 6 and 7, and getting 'long' backs me into 9, not ideal either!

Above: *The Corkscrew manoeuvre. Reds 6 and 7 fly inverted as Reds 8 and 9 barrel roll around their smoke trails.*

Opposite: *Painting shapes in the sky. The team leaves a beautiful arc of smoke in the clear blue sky. A perfect day for display flying.*

"... the Corkscrew manoeuvre ... involves Reds 6 and 7 flying level upside down along the length of the crowd with me about three aeroplane lengths behind barrel rolling around their smoke ..."

Above: The Corkscrew in close up. Reds 6 and 7 (the Synchro Pair) have rolled inverted together and are trailing white smoke.

Above: The view from Red 7 in the Corkscrew, with Red 6 filling the field of view. Upside down and close – challenging flying!

Above: The view ahead from Red 8 as he rolls around 6 and 7's smoke in the Corkscrew.

Above: Still rolling around the smoke in the Corkscrew, Red 8 gets as close to the smoke trails as possible, sometimes buffeting through the wake turbulence from the aircraft ahead.

RADIO CALLS

Diamond go

Call from the leader to instruct the pilots to change to this formation. Call is applied to all formations and changes appropriately, i.e. 'Shuttle go'. Instruction will be acknowledged by the pilots moving formation.

Smoke on go

The famous call from the leader for smoke. There is a particular smoke plot for every different formation or manoeuvre. The pilots have to remember each one and get the smoke right every time.

Gypo going full

Call from Red 6, 'Gypo' leader, that they are changing to a Full Display routine. Likely if the weather has improved. Changes to flat and rolling displays may also be called. Red 1 makes these calls for 'Enid'.

Coming left now

Call from the leader to let the formation know he is turning left. 'Coming right now' used for turns to the right.

Holding the bank now

Leader letting the formation know that he has reached the desired angle of bank for the turn.

Tightening

Call from the leader to let the formation know he is tightening the turn. It is usually a 3G turn in the big formation.

Letting it out

Call from the leader to let the formation know he is relaxing the backpressure on the stick in the turn. So, decreasing the turn rate.

Rolling out

Leader letting the formation know that he is rolling the formation level and ending the turn.

Pulling up
Call from the leader that he is pulling back on the stick and climbing the formation into a loop or roll.

Above: In the Boss' jet during the steep climb. Reds 2 and 4 are on the leader's right, with 3 and 5 on the leader's left.

Above right: Lined up on the runway and ready to roll. 'Reds rolling, now!'

" ... Gypo going full: call from Red 6, 'Gypo' leader, that they are changing to Full Display routine ... Likely if the weather has improved ..."

Riding with the Reds:
The photographer's view

As a passenger I 'walk' to my allocated Hawk jet well in advance of the nine team pilots to ensure I am strapped in and ready when they arrive. The pilots get to their aircraft with only minutes to spare. They quickly don their G-suits, life-saving jackets and helmets, and strap into the Hawks in very short order – ready to meet the required split second timing of the flight, which starts with a pre-determined check-in time. 'Reds check, 2, 3, 4, 5, 6, 7, 8, 9. Scampton tower, Red Arrows, nine aircraft ready to taxi'.

As the Boss checks us in with the tower, I put my dark visor down and raise my oxygen mask as my pilot, Red 7 Flt Lt Mike Ling, checks I am ready to close the canopy. The MDC (Miniature Detonation Cord) in the canopy can potentially fire on closing so every care is taken, even closing your eyes is part of the drill. I have already dialled my weight into the ejection seat and lowered it to ensure I have a fist's worth of clearance between my white Mk10B helmet and the canopy. We taxi in order and line up on the runway – the adrenalin is already starting to flow and I am just a passenger taking photos.

'Display take-off coming left'. The call from the leader comes as we line up at intervals along the runway. 'Reds rolling…now'. With full power applied the pilots release the brakes and we roll down the runway as one. 'Lingy' releases his brakes on a cue from 'Baz' Murphy in Red 6. As he signals with a pronounced nod of the head we are off. With my feet sitting lightly on the rudder pedals, the inputs come thick and fast from my pilot as he

Above: *The Hawk's airbrake is a vital part of formation flying for the team. It is quicker to use a dab of airbrake than to throttle back and then power back up because of the time it takes the engine to spool down or up. This is a typical team pilot's view of the aircraft ahead.*

Left: *In the Mirror roll, photographed from Red 8. The lowest aircraft is Red 7 – note how hard he is having to crane his neck to formate on Red 6, who is inverted directly above him. Of additional note is the backseater. He is E. J. van Koningsveld, long-time friend and civilian photographer for the team.*

Opposite: *As a photographer, experience tells you when to capture remarkable moments in the display, and also when to stow your camera out of the way and prepare for high G-forces.*

"… a balance of power, airbrake, rudder and stick are what these highly skilled pilots use to hold this tight position …"

keeps the Hawk perfectly straight on the runway as we swiftly accelerate in formation with the aircraft ahead. Once airborne the nine Hawks immediately move into tight diamond formation – this really is close, rock-solid formation flying and the pilots are all working incredibly hard. A balance of power, airbrake, rudder and stick are what these highly skilled pilots use to hold this tight position. We are cleared into a full practice display. 'Smoke on…go!' 'Coming right…now', 'Holding the bank…now', 'Tightening'. The calls from the leader come thick and fast.

The silent passenger

As a photographer passenger it is crucial that the pilot doesn't feel you in the back seat; you never ever knock the control column by mistake, that could be inviting disaster. The 'tightening' call from the leader signals that G is coming on in the turn, only about 3G but enough to mean I need to brace or stow my Nikon D3 camera up on the instrument panel in front of me. 'Letting it out'. This call means that the leader is relaxing the pull in the turn and the G comes off. For the first half of the display it is a sequence of turns and loops in changing formations.

The work rate for the pilots is extraordinary throughout the entire flight. The dark helmet visors of the nine pilots mask the immense concentration and workload required to stay on the wings of the leader as they paint the sky with red, white and blue smoke in their looping, rolling and breaking manoeuvres. As we finish the first half and split into 'Enid' and 'Gypo', it's time for the more dynamic second half of the display. Meanwhile, I am in the back,

working hard to capture as many exhilarating moments of the display as possible, punctuated by some aggressive, chest-crushing flying. After a sweat-soaked 30 minutes we are running in over the airfield for one last formation break before we all land in turn. One last G-saturated pull and we are ready for landing. A quick check from 'Lingy' that my toes are clear of the brakes and we turn finals to grease down on the runway. Now the sweat is really pouring off me, so goodness knows how the pilots have remained so cool.

As we taxi, in I am cleared to replace my ejection seat and canopy safety pins and, as we come to a halt, we are met by the dedicated groundcrews. As the canopy opens, the engines have already spooled down and 'Lingy' is climbing out. 'See you inside', he says, as the engineers waste no time swinging into action to prepare the jets for the next practice.

The pilots immediately go into a detailed team debrief, making full use of the excellent video that is filmed from the ground for every display. This is a vital tool for the pilots and while watching the video they are very hard on themselves. Calls of 'short', 'long', 'shallow', 'deep' from various members of the team indicate how they feel their positioning was within each formation. Sitting in the debrief I struggle to see the errors, but these pilots are talking about literally inches of difference in positioning. For me as a photographer, it is a huge privilege and challenge to try to capture this incredible experience and give some insight into the team. In the words of the Red Arrows' motto: 'Eclat' – brilliance.

Opposite above: *The Gypo Pass, an impressive crossover by Reds 6-9. Closing head on at nearly 1000mph (left). The Gypo Break, seen from the cockpit of Red 8. Reds 6 and 7 are crossing ahead (centre). The view from Red 8 closing in on 'Enid' formation for the Goose (right).*

Opposite below: *A pilot's eye view of the aircraft directly ahead in the formation as the team dives out of a loop.*

"... after a sweat-soaked 30 minutes we are running in over the airfield for one last formation break ... the sweat is pouring off me, so goodness knows how the pilots have remained so cool ..."

Opposite: The Gypo Break in detail. Reds 6 and 7 are closer to the camera, with Reds 8 and 9 to the rear.

Above: Viewed from head on you get the impression that all four aircraft are going to hit, but actually they are cleverly staggered, which allows the crossovers and their impressive smoke trails to be performed in safety. Note the vortices streaming from the wingtips, illustrating that this manoeuvre involves a break at 8G.

Following pages left: Looking ahead at the formation through the canopy. This shot clearly illustrates just how close the aircraft are flying in formation.

Following pages right: The impressive Mirror Roll. Red 6 is the leading aircraft for this – he is flying inverted. Red 7 is directly below 6, flying formation on him. Reds 8 and 9 are formating on Red 6 but they are flying right way up. This clearly illustrates the procedures in place to ensure that everyone is holding formation position on the correct aircraft and who is avoiding whom.

TEAM

'Reds, Break, Break…Go!'

Appendices

Team members

Red Arrows display pilots, Red 10s, Team Managers, Engineering Officers, Public Relations Managers and Adjutants.

2009
Leader Wg Cdr J R Hawker
2 Flt Lt Z Sennett
3 Flt Lt D Montenegro
4 Flt Lt D Davies
5 Flt Lt S P Rea
6 Sqn Ldr B D Murphy
7 Flt Lt M R Ling
8 Sqn Ldr G Duff
9 Flt Lt A R Keith
10 Sqn Ldr G Bagnall
Manager Sqn Ldr J S Trott
PRM Nikki Wright
SEngO Sqn Ldr G Ball
JEngO Flt Lt C Fenn
Adjutant WO A Murray

2008
Leader Wg Cdr J R Hawker
2 Flt Lt S P Rea
3 Flt Lt M R Ling
4 Sqn Ldr G Duff
5 Flt Lt A R Keith
6 Flt Lt P O'Grady
7 Sqn Ldr B D Murphy
8 Flt Lt G B J Perilleux
9 Flt Lt D R Ellacott
10 Flt Lt A C R Robins
Manager Sqn Ldr J S Trott
PRM Miss R L Huxford
SEngO Sqn Ldr E D Williams
JEngO Flt Lt C Fenn
Adjutant WO J H May

2007
Leader Wg Cdr J R Hawker
2 Sqn Ldr B Murphy
3 Flt Lt A Keith
4 Flt Lt G Perilleux
5 Flt Lt D Ellacott
6 Sqn Ldr J H Turner
7 Flt Lt P O'Grady
8 Sqn Ldr S Morley
9 Sqn Ldr M Higgins
10 Flt Lt A Robins
Manager Sqn Ldr P J Hunt
PRO Miss R L Huxford
SEngO Sqn Ldr E D Williams
JEngO Flt Lt A Scott
Adjutant WO J H May

2006
Leader Wg Cdr R P G Patounas
2 Flt Lt G B J Perilleux
3 Flt Lt D R Ellacott
4 Sqn Ldr S Morley
5 Flt Lt P O'Grady
6 Flt Lt S D Stevens
7 Flt Lt J H Turner
8 Flt Lt D J Slow
9 Sqn Ldr M J Higgins
10 Flt Lt A C R Robins
Manager Sqn Ldr P J Hunt
PRO Miss R L Huxford
SEngO Sqn Ldr S R Davies
JEngO Flt Lt R D J Gates
Adjutant WO J H May

2005
Leader Sqn Ldr R P G Patounas
2 Flt Lt S Morley
3 Flt Lt M J Higgins
4 Flt Lt D J Slow
5 Flt Lt J H Turner

6 Sqn Ldr D J Simmons
7 Flt Lt S D Stevens
8 Flt Lt J P Griggs
9 Sqn Ldr D C Mason
10 Flt Lt S C Underwood
Manager Sqn Ldr S E Varley
PRO Miss R L Huxford
SEngO Sqn Ldr S R Davies
JEngO Flt Lt S C Race
Adjutant WO J H May

2004
Leader Sqn Ldr C D Jepson
2 Flt Lt A F Parkinson
3 Flt Lt S D Stevens
4 Flt Lt D J Slow
5 Sqn Ldr D C Mason
6 Sqn Ldr D Thomas
7 Flt Lt D J Simmons
8 Flt Lt J P Griggs
9 Sqn Ldr J H Green
10 Flt Lt S C Underwood
Manager Sqn Ldr S E Varley
PRO Miss R L Huxford
SEngO Sqn Ldr R K Carleton
JEngO Flt Lt S C Race
Adjutant WO J H May

2003
Leader Sqn Ldr C D Jepson
2 Flt Lt J P Griggs
3 Flt Lt D C Mason
4 Flt Lt D J Simmons
5 Sqn Ldr J H Green
6 Sqn Ldr M M Garland
7 Sqn Ldr D Thomas
8 Flt Lt A F Parkinson
9 Sqn Ldr C Gleave
10 Flt Lt S C Underwood
Manager Sqn Ldr S E Varley

PRO Miss R L Huxford
SEngO Sqn Ldr R K Carleton
JEngO Flt Lt T Beagle
Adjutant WO J H May

2002
Leader Sqn Ldr C D Jepson
2 Flt Lt D Thomas
3 Sqn Ldr J H Green
4 Flt Lt A F Parkinson
5 Sqn Ldr C Gleave
6 Sqn Ldr J R Hawker
7 Sqn Ldr M M Garland
8 Sqn Ldr C D Carder
9 Flt Lt J P Hughes
10 Flt Lt S C Underwood
Manager Sqn Ldr L C Johnson
SEngO Sqn Ldr M J Northover
JEngO Flt Lt T Beagle
Adjutant WO J H May

2001
Leader Wg Cdr A C Offer
2 Flt Lt A F Parkinson
3 Flt Lt C Gleave
4 Sqn Ldr M M Garland
5 Flt Lt J P Hughes
6 Sqn Ldr J D Provost
7 Flt Lt J R Hawker
8 Sqn Ldr C D Carder
9 Flt Lt M R Cutmore
10 Sqn Ldr A D E Evans
Manager Sqn Ldr J M Paige
SEngO Sqn Ldr M J Northover
JEngO Flt Lt T Beagle
Adjutant WO J H May

Opposite: Throughout its history, the Red Arrows has been a team renowned as being truly a British icon. The team is something that the British public can be justly proud of.

2000

Leader Sqn Ldr A C Offer
2 Flt Lt J R Hawker
3 Flt Lt J P Hughes
4 Flt Lt C D Carder
5 Flt Lt M R Cutmore
6 Flt Lt R P G Patounas
7 Flt Lt J D Provost
8 Flt Lt A D E Evans
9 Sqn Ldr K A Lewis
10 Flt Lt R R Jones
Manager Sqn Ldr J M Paige
SEngO Sqn Ldr M J Northover
JEngO Flt Lt A D McNeill
Adjutant WO J H May

1999

Leader Wg Cdr S C Meade
2 Flt Lt J D Provost
3 Flt Lt M R Cutmore
4 Flt Lt A D E Evans
5 Sqn Ldr K A Lewis
6 Sqn Ldr A Cubin
7 Flt Lt R P G Patounas
8 Flt Lt I S Smith
9 Sqn Ldr G M Waterfall
10 Flt Lt R R Jones
Manager Sqn Ldr J M Paige
SEngO Flt Lt G Martin
JEngO Flt Lt A D McNeill
Adjutant WO J Howard

1998

Leader Sqn Ldr S C Meade
2 Flt Lt A D E Evans
3 Flt Lt K A Lewis
4 Flt Lt I S Smith
5 Flt Lt R P G Patounas
6 Flt Lt D N Stobie
7 Flt Lt A Cubin
8 Sqn Ldr A C Offer
9 Sqn Ldr G M Waterfall
10 Flt Lt R R Jones
Manager Sqn Ldr E E Webster
SEngO Flt Lt D Chowns
JEngO Flt Lt J Russell
Adjutant WO J Howard

1997

Leader Sqn Ldr S C Meade
2 Flt Lt I S Smith
3 Flt Lt G M Waterfall
4 Sqn Ldr A C Offer
5 Flt Lt A Cubin
6 Flt Lt T Couston

7 Flt Lt D N Stobie
8 Flt Lt R Matthews
9 Flt Lt S D Perrett
Manager Sqn Ldr H M Williams
SEngO Flt Lt D Chowns
JEngO Flt Lt J Russell
Adjutant WO J Howard

1996

Leader Sqn Ldr J E Rands
2 Sqn Ldr A C Offer
3 Flt Lt D N Stobie
4 Flt Lt R Matthews
5 Flt Lt S D Perrett
6 Sqn Ldr K P Truss
7 Flt Lt T Couston
8 Flt Lt C D Jepson
9 Flt Lt M W Zanker
Manager Sqn Ldr H M Williams
Engineer Flt Lt M J Northover
Adjutant WO J Howard

1995

Leader Sqn Ldr J E Rands
2 Flt Lt R Matthews
3 Flt Lt S D Perrett
4 Flt Lt T Couston
5 Flt Lt M W Zanker
6 Flt Lt S Chiddention
7 Sqn Ldr K P Truss
8 Flt Lt C D Jepson
9 Sqn Ldr M G Ball
Manager Sqn Ldr H M Williams
Engineer Flt Lt M J Northover
Adjutant WO J Howard

1994

Leader Sqn Ldr J E Rands
2 Flt Lt C D Jepson
3 Flt Lt M W Zanker
4 Flt Lt K P Truss
5 Flt Lt M G Ball
6 Flt Lt R W Last
7 Flt Lt S Chiddention
8 Flt Lt B J Cross
9 Flt Lt J C Bird
Manager Sqn Ldr L Garside-
    Beattie
Engineer Flt Lt M J Northover
Adjutant WO J Howard

1993

Leader Sqn Ldr A P Thurley
2 Flt Lt S Chiddention
3 Flt Lt M G Ball

4 Flt Lt B J Cross
5 Flt Lt J C Bird
6 Sqn Ldr S C Meade
7 Flt Lt R W Last
8 Sqn Ldr G P Howes
9 Flt Lt N C Rogers
Manager Sqn Ldr L Garside-
    Beattie
Engineer Flt Lt R L Miller
Adjutant WO J Howard

1992

Leader Sqn Ldr A P Thurley
2 Flt Lt R W Last
3 Flt Lt B J Cross
4 Sqn Ldr G P Howes
5 Flt Lt J C Bird
6 Sqn Ldr D A Wyatt
7 Flt Lt S C Meade
8 Flt Lt A Smith
9 Flt Lt N C Rogers
Manager Sqn Ldr L Garside-
    Beattie
Engineer Flt Lt R L Miller
Adjutant WO M R J Fleckney

1991

Leader Sqn Ldr A P Thurley
2 Flt Lt G P Howes
3 Flt Lt N C Rogers
4 Flt Lt A Smith
5 Flt Lt S C Meade
6 Flt Lt J M Newton
7 Flt Lt D A Wyatt
8 Flt Lt A W Hoy
9 Flt Lt M J H Cliff
Manager Sqn Ldr A J Stewart
Engineer Flt Lt C R Bushell
Adjutant WO M R J Fleckney

1990

Leader Sqn Ldr T W L Miller
2 Flt Lt A Smith
3 Flt Lt P C H Rogers
4 Flt Lt A W Hoy
5 Sqn Ldr D C Riley
6 Flt Lt S W M Johnson
7 Flt Lt J M Newton
8 Flt Lt D A Wyatt
9 Flt Lt M J H Cliff
Manager Sqn Ldr A J Stewart
Engineer Flt Lt C R Bushell
Adjutant WO M R J Fleckney

1989

Leader Sqn Ldr T W L Miller
2 Flt Lt A W Hoy
3 Flt Lt M J H Cliff
4 Flt Lt G M Bancroft-Wilson
5 Sqn Ldr D C Riley
6 Flt Lt J E Rands
7 Flt Lt S W M Johnson
8 Flt Lt J W Glover
9 Flt Lt M J M Newton
Manager Sqn Ldr A J Stewart
Engineer Flt Lt J D Williams
Adjutant WO M R J Fleckney

1988

Leader Sqn Ldr T W L Miller
2 Flt Lt G M Bancroft-Wilson
3 Flt Lt D C Riley
4 Sqn Ldr P J Collins
5 Flt Lt S W M Johnson
6 Sqn Ldr A P Thurley
7 Flt Lt J E Rands
8 Sqn Ldr J W Glover
9 Flt Lt M A Carter
Manager Sqn Ldr H R Ploszek
Engineer Flt Lt J D Williams
Adjutant WO M R J Fleckney

1987

Leader Sqn Ldr R M Thomas
2 Sqn Ldr P J Collins
3 Flt Lt M A Carter
4 Flt Lt M J Newbery
5 Sqn Ldr A B Chubb
6 Flt Lt C D R McIlroy
7 Flt Lt A P Thurley
8 Flt Lt J E Rands
9 Flt Lt G M Bancroft-Wilson
Manager Sqn Ldr H R Ploszek
Engineer Flt Lt J S Chantry
Adjutant WO M R J Fleckney

1986

Leader Sqn Ldr R M Thomas
2 Flt Lt P D Lees
3 Sqn Ldr A B Chubb
4 Flt Lt P J Collins
5 Sqn Ldr G I Hannam
6 Flt Lt A K Lunnon-Wood
7 Flt Lt C D R McIlroy
8 Flt Lt D W Findlay
9 Flt Lt A P Thurley
Manager Sqn Ldr H R Ploszek
Engineer Flt Lt J S Chantry
Adjutant WO D H A Chubb

1985

Leader Sqn Ldr R M Thomas
2 Flt Lt P D Lees
3 Sqn Ldr E H Ball
4 Flt Lt S H Bedford
5 Sqn Ldr G I Hannam
6 Flt Lt A R Boyens
7 Flt Lt A K Lunnon-Wood
8 Flt Lt C D R McIlroy
9 Sqn Ldr A B Chubb
Manager Sqn Ldr H R Ploszek
Engineer Flt Lt M E J Render
Adjutant WO D H A Chubb

1984

Leader Sqn Ldr J Blackwell
2 Flt Lt S H Bedford
3 Flt Lt G I Hannam
4 Sqn Ldr T W L Miller
5 Sqn Ldr E H Ball
6 Flt Lt P A Tolman
7 Flt Lt A R Boyens
8 Flt Lt P D Lees
9 Flt Lt A K Lunnon-Wood
Manager Sqn Ldr J E Steenson
Engineer Flt Lt M E J Render
Adjutant WO D H A Chubb

1983

Leader Sqn Ldr J Blackwell
2 Sqn Ldr I J Huzzard
3 Flt Lt J R Myers
4 Flt Lt T W L Miller
5 Flt Lt E H Ball
6 Flt Lt M H de Courcier
7 Flt Lt P A Tolman
8 Flt Lt S H Bedford
9 Flt Lt C A R Hirst
Manager Sqn Ldr J E Steenson
Engineer Flt Lt M E J Render
Adjutant WO H G Thorne

1982

Leader Sqn Ldr J Blackwell
2 Flt Lt B S Walters
3 Flt Lt J R Myers
4 Flt Lt I J Huzzard
5 Flt Lt W Ward
6 Flt Lt T R Watts
7 Flt Lt M H de Courcier
8 Flt Lt T W L Miller
9 Flt Lt P A Tolman
Manager Sqn Ldr R Thilthorpe
Engineer Flt Lt G M Nisbet
Adjutant WO H G Thorne

1981

Leader Sqn Ldr B R Hoskins
2 Flt Lt B F Walters
3 Flt Lt W Ward
4 Flt Lt M H de Courcier
5 Flt Lt N J Wharton
6 Sqn Ldr S R Johnson
7 Flt Lt T R Watts
8 Flt Lt I J Huzzard
9 Flt Lt J R Myers
Manager Sqn Ldr R Thilthorpe
Engineer Flt Lt G M Nisbet
Adjutant WO H G Thorne

1980

Leader Sqn Ldr B R Hoskins
2 Flt Lt M D Howell
3 Flt Lt W Ward
4 Flt Lt N J Wharton
5 Flt Lt B C Scott
6 Flt Lt R M Thomas
7 Sqn Ldr S R Johnson
8 Flt Lt B S Walters
9 Flt Lt T R Watts
Manager Sqn Ldr R Thilthorpe
Engineer Flt Lt R A Lewis
Adjutant WO H G Thorne

1979

Leader Sqn Ldr B R Hoskins
2 Flt Lt M T Curley
3 Flt Lt B C Scott
4 Flt Lt M D Howell
5 Flt Lt M B Stoner
6 Flt Lt R M Thomas
7 Sqn Ldr S R Johnson
8 Flt Lt N J Wharton
9 Flt Lt W Ward
Manager Sqn Ldr R Thilthorpe
Engineer Flt Lt R A Lewis
Adjutant WO H G Thorne

1978

Leader Sqn Ldr F J Hoare
2 Flt Lt D R Carvell
3 Flt Lt M B Stoner
4 Flt Lt M J Phillips
5 Flt Lt L A Grose
6 Flt Lt M T Curley
7 Flt Lt R M Thomas
8 Flt Lt S R Johnson
9 Flt Lt B C Scott
Manager Flt Lt M B Whitehouse
Engineer Flt Lt R A Lewis
Adjutant WO H G Thorne

1977
Leader Sqn Ldr F J Hoare
2 Flt Lt D R Carvell
3 Flt Lt R S Barber
4 Flt Lt M J Phillips
5 Flt Lt N S Champness
6 Flt Lt M Cornwell
7 Flt Lt M T Curley
8 Flt Lt R M Thomas
9 Flt Lt M B Stoner
Manager Flt Lt M B Whitehouse
Engineer Flt Lt A Hunt
Adjutant WO H G Thorne

1976
Leader Sqn Ldr R B Duckett
2 Flt Lt M J Phillips
3 Flt Lt R Eccles
4 Flt Lt D R Carvell
5 Flt Lt R S Barber
6 Sqn Ldr B R Hoskins
7 Flt Lt M Cornwell
8 Flt Lt M T Curley
9 Flt Lt N S Champness
Manager Sqn Ldr A L Wall
Engineer Flt Lt A Hunt
Adjutant WO H G Thorne

1975
Leader Sqn Ldr R B Duckett
2 Flt Lt M J Phillips
3 Flt Lt B Donnelly
4 Flt Lt R Eccles
5 Flt Lt J Blackwell
6 Flt Lt D Sheen
7 Sqn Ldr B R Hoskins
8 Flt Lt M Cornwell
9 Flt Lt R Barber
Manager Sqn Ldr A L Wall
Engineer Flt Lt A Hunt
Adjutant WO H E D Runsdstrom

1974
Leader Sqn Ldr I C H Dick
2 Flt Lt K J Tait
3 Flt Lt B Donnelly
4 Flt Lt E E G Girdler
5 Flt Lt C M Phillips
6 Flt Lt D Binnie
7 Sqn Ldr R E Somerville
8 Flt Lt D J Sheen
9 Flt Lt R Eccles
Manager Flt Lt R M Joy
Engineer Flt Lt I Brackenbury
Adjutant WO H E D Runsdstrom

1973
Leader Sqn Ldr I C H Dick
2 Sqn Ldr W B Aspinall
3 Flt Lt B Donnelly
4 Flt Lt E E G Girdler
5 Flt Lt K J Tait
6 Flt Lt D Binnie
7 Sqn Ldr R E Somerville
8 Flt Lt D J Sheen
9 Flt Lt P J J Day
Manager Flt Lt R M Joy
Engineer Flt Lt I Brackenbury
Adjutant WO H E D Runsdstrom

1972
Leader Sqn Ldr I C H Dick
2 Flt Lt W B Aspinall
3 Flt Lt A C East
4 Flt Lt R E Somerville
5 Flt Lt K J Tait
6 Flt Lt P J J Day
7 Flt Lt D Binnie
8 Flt Lt E E G Girdler
9 Flt Lt C F Roberts
Manager Flt Lt B Donnelly
Engineer Flt Lt I Brackenbury
Adjutant WO S Wild

1971
Leader Sqn Ldr R E W Loverseed
2 Sqn Ldr D S B Marr
3 Flt Lt A C East
4 Flt Lt W B Aspinall
5 Flt Lt P J J Day
6 Flt Lt C F Roberts
7 Flt Lt R E Somerville
Manager Flt Lt K J Tait
Engineer Flt Lt G E White
Adjutant WO L Ludlow

1970
Leader Sqn Ldr D Hazell
2 Flt Lt R Perreaux
3 Flt Lt D A Smith
4 Flt Lt J D Rust
5 Flt Lt J Haddock
6 Flt Lt I C H Dick
7 Flt Lt R B Duckett
8 Flt Lt D S B Marr
9 Flt Lt R E W Loverseed
Manager Flt Lt P Mackintosh
Engineer Flt Lt G E White
Adjutant WO L Ludlow

1969
Leader Sqn Ldr R G Hanna
2 Flt Lt P R Evans
3 Flt Lt D A Smith
4 Flt Lt R B Duckett
5 Flt Lt E R Perreaux
6 Flt Lt J T Kingsley
7 Flt Lt I C H Dick
8 Flt Lt J D Rust
9 Sqn Ldr R P Dunn
Manager Flt Lt P Mackintosh
Engineer Fg Off G E White
Adjutant Flt Lt R Dench

1968
Leader Sqn Ldr R G Hanna
2 Flt Lt D A Bell
3 Flt Lt D A Smith
4 Flt Lt P R Evans
5 Flt Lt F J Hoare
6 Flt Lt R Booth
7 Flt Lt J T Kingsley
8 Flt Lt I C H Dick
9 Flt Lt R B Duckett
Manager Flt Lt L G Wilcox
Engineer Fg Off D Whitby
Adjutant Flt Lt R Dench

1967
Leader Sqn Ldr R G Hanna
2 Flt Lt D A Bell
3 Flt Lt F J Hoare
4 Flt Lt P R Evans
5 Flt Lt R Booth
6 Flt Lt H J D Prince
7 Flt Lt E E Jones
Manager Flt Lt L G Wilcox
Engineer Fg Off D Whitby
Adjutant Flt Lt R Dench

1966
Leader Sqn Ldr R G Hanna
2 Flt Lt D A Bell
3 Flt Lt R W Langworthy
4 Flt Lt P R Evans
5 Flt Lt R Booth
6 Flt Lt H J D Prince
7 Flt Lt T J G Nelson
8 Flt Lt F J Hoare
9 Flt Lt D McGregor
Manager Sqn Ldr R A E Storer
Engineer Fg Off C T Harrow
Engineer Fg Off D Whitby

1965
Leader Flt Lt L Jones
2 Flt Lt B A Nice
3 Flt Lt R G Hanna
4 Flt Lt G L Ranscombe
5 Fg Off P G Hay
6 Flt Lt R E W Loverseed
7 Flt Lt H J D Prince
8 Flt Lt E C F Tilsley
Manager Sqn Ldr R A E Storer
Engineer Fg Off D Green
Engineer Fg Off C T Harrow
Engineer Fg Off D Whitby

Current aircraft

The Red Arrows operate 13 BAE Systems Hawk T1 aircraft:
XX179 - Joined the team in April 2002
XX227 - Founder aircraft (with the team since 1980)
XX233 - Joined the team in 1988 from 4 FTS
XX237 - First used by Reds in 1985
XX242 - Joined the team in 2003 from RAF Valley
XX253 - Founder aircraft
XX260 - Founder aircraft
XX264 - Founder aircraft
XX266 - Founder aircraft
XX292 - Joined the team in 1996 from 4FTS
XX294 - Joined the team in 1988 from 4FTS
XX306 - Founder aircraft
XX308 - Joined the team in 1985

Acknowledgements

A book such as this is only made possible by the vital contribution of numerous people. The author wishes to express his sincere thanks to the many individuals who have allowed him this highly privileged opportunity.

In particular, Wg Cdr Jas Hawker for allowing me the opportunity to produce the book and for his authorisation of many unique opportunities that help make this volume so special.

Sqn Ldr Jon Trott helped organise many visits to RAF Scampton and co-ordinated so many of the finer points necessary to produce a book. He was generally pivotal in making this project work.

I must also thank Wg Cdr Dicky Patounas for first allowing me to work with the team officially in 2005 and Phill O'Dell for the introduction. Many thanks also to Sqn Ldr Graham Duff and Charlie McIlroy for penning their splendid and fascinating recollections. Plus all members of the team past and present who have assisted me including the members of Circus, the Blues and the survival equipment fitters.

Thanks also to my friend and fellow photographer E. J. van Koningsveld for many hours in the crewroom trading ideas and formulating plans. Thanks to John McDonald of Nikon Professional UK for his help and support.

Thanks also to Sue Pressley and Paul Turner of Touchstone Books for creating this wonderful book to showcase everyone's hard work and to my wife Claire for all her encouragement and support.

Air Chief Marshal Stephen Dalton
Group Captain Nick Seward, Commandant Central Flying School
Group Captain Nicky Loveday, RAF Corporate Communications
Group Captain Steve Ayres
Wg Cdr Jas Hawker
Wg Cdr Dicky Patounas
Wg Cdr Dave Middleton
Wg Cdr David Firth-Wigglesworth
Sqn Ldr Graham Duff
Sqn Ldr Scott Morley
Sqn Ldr Martin Higgins
Sqn Ldr Ben Murphy
Sqn Ldr Jon Trott
Sqn Ldr Paula Hunt
Sqn Ldr Jim Turner
Sqn Ldr Sally Varley
Sqn Ldr Simon Race
Sqn Ldr Simon Davies
Sqn Ldr Ed Williams
Flt Lt Si Stevens
Flt Lt Mike Ling
Flt Lt Pablo O'Grady
Flt Lt Simon Rea
Flt Lt Andrew Keith
Flt Lt Greg Perilleux
Flt Lt Damo Ellacott
Flt Lt Andy Robins
Flt Lt Zane Sennett
Flt Lt Dave Davies
Flt Lt David Montenegro
Flt Lt Charlotte Fenn
Flt Lt Alison Scott
Flt Lt Steve Underwood
WO John May
WO Alan Murray
Rachel Huxford
Emma Thomas
Nikki Wright
Flt Sgt Steve Cox
Sgt Paul Brown
Cpl Andy Benson
Cpl Paul Richardson
Cpl Dave Wright
Cpl Mick Nicholson
Cpl Pete Jones
Cpl Simon Evans
Cpl Phil Ackerley
Cpl Alex Heaton
Cpl Mark Heath
Cpl Pete Targett
Cpl Ben Stevenson
SAC Adam Foster
SAC Stuart Chapman
SAC Peter Lamb
SAC Liam O'Keeffe
SAC Rob Wheeler
SAC James Burdett
SAC Ben Stevenson
SAC Simon Miller
SAC Ann Muldowney
E. J. van Koningsveld
Charlie McIlroy
Phill O'Dell, Chief Test Pilot, Rolls-Royce
Mike Nixon, Rolls-Royce
Nick Britton, Rolls-Royce
Kate Watcham, BAE Systems

Red Arrows Full Display Sequence 2009

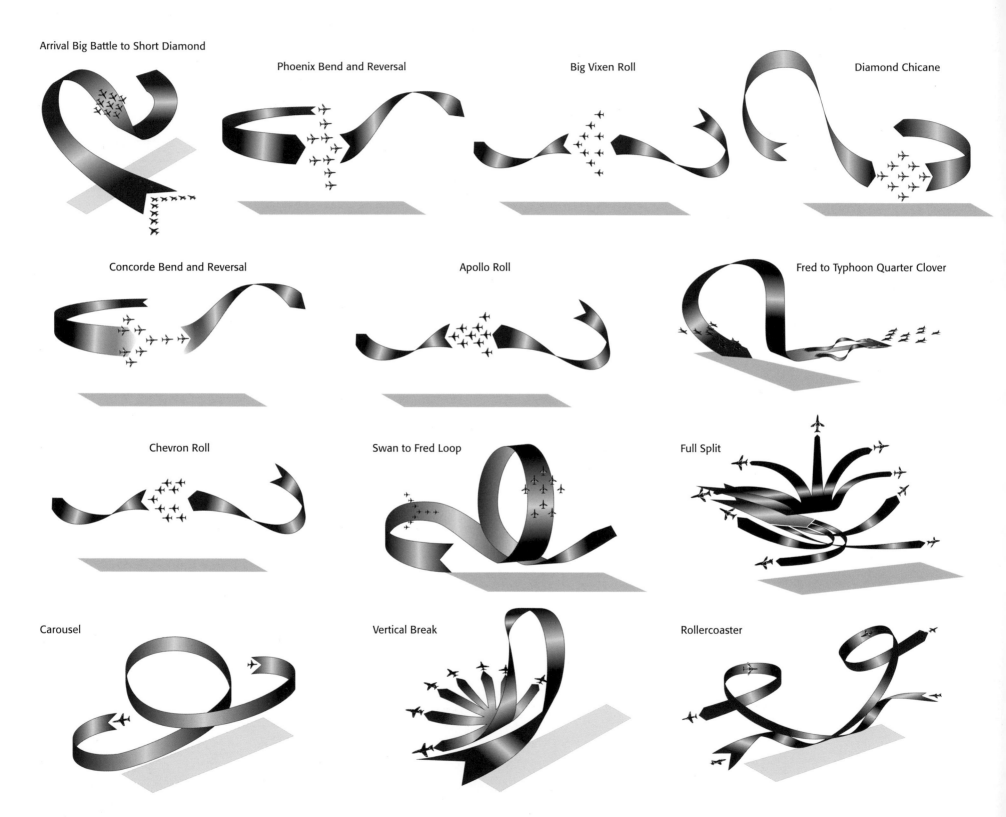

Arrival Big Battle to Short Diamond

Phoenix Bend and Reversal

Big Vixen Roll

Diamond Chicane

Concorde Bend and Reversal

Apollo Roll

Fred to Typhoon Quarter Clover

Chevron Roll

Swan to Fred Loop

Full Split

Carousel

Vertical Break

Rollercoaster

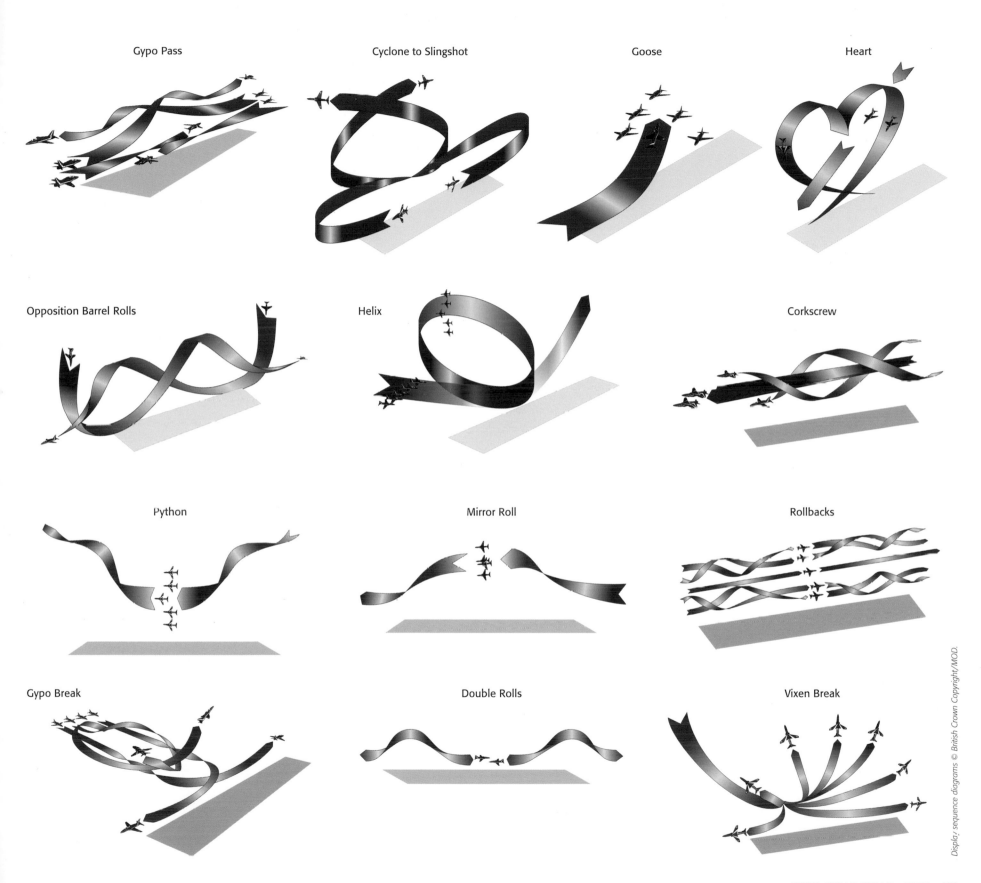

Gypo Pass

Cyclone to Slingshot

Goose

Heart

Opposition Barrel Rolls

Helix

Corkscrew

Python

Mirror Roll

Rollbacks

Gypo Break

Double Rolls

Vixen Break

Display sequence diagrams © British Crown Copyright/MOD.

Index

administration team 7, 143
airshows 43, 48, 50, 64, 92, 126, 127, 139
Ackerley, Phil (Cpl) 92, 101
aerobatic display teams 43

BAE Systems 109, 110, 120–121
Bagnall, Graeme (Sqn Ldr) 126
Ball, Garry (Sqn Ldr) 89
Battle of Britain Memorial Flight 50
Bedford, Andy (Flt Sgt) 92
Bedford, Simon 45
Black Arrows 43
Blues 7, 24, 89, 91, 139, 143
British Airways Concorde 48
British Aerospace 43, 109
Brown, Paul (Sgt) 89, 105
Budziszewski, Darren (Cpl) 10

Central Flying School (CFS) 43, 109
Chapman, Stu (SAC) 100
charity work 12, 25
Circus 7, 89, 91, 92, 92, 98, 100, 128
    leader 90
cockpit 101, 110, 112, 114
Conway, Dan (SAC) 91, 101
Cox, Steve (Flt Sgt) 89
Cubin, Andy 50
Cyprus 34, 48, 60, 63, 99, 101, 107, 110,
    126, 127, 130, 133, 149

Dalton, Stephen (Air Chief Marshal) 7
Davies, Dave (Flt Lt) 72, 76, 91, 112
Derry, John 53
Diamond Nine 7, 46, 53, 61
displays 23, 24, 30, 43, 44, 50, 54, 56, 66,
    67, 72, 73, 75, 96, 99, 106, 109, 126,
    130, 134, 135, 147–169, 174–175
Duff, Graham (Sqn Ldr) 54, 55, 56, 59, 62,
    114, 128, 139, 156
Duke, Neville 53
dye team 96, 100, 106, 107

Eclat (brilliance) 9, 165
ejection seat 90, 112, 114, 165
Ellacott, Damo (Flt Lt) 54, 59, 84
Elton, Tim (Cpl) 105
Empire Test Pilot School (ETPS) 60, 63
engineers 24, 89, 90, 96, 99, 101, 104, 105
'Enid Uncle' 83
Eurofighter Typhoon 23

Evans, Simon (Cpl) 143
Events Team 24
'Exec' 83, 132

Fenn, Charlotte (Flt Lt) 12, 67, 89, 143
Firth-Wigglesworth, David (Wg Cdr) 83
Folland Gnat 9, 43, 44, 50, 109
formations and manoeuvres 25, 29, 39, 46,
    67, 68, 69, 70, 72, 80, 83, 84, 106, 136,
    147–169, 174-175
    Apollo 46
    Big Battle 24, 127, 130
    Big Vixen 20, 46
    Bomb Burst 46
    Caterpillar 149
    Concorde 46, 70
    Corkscrew Roll 83, 149, 155, 156, 158,
        159
    crossover 25, 46, 147, 149
    Delta Roll 46
    Derry Turn 80
    Diamond Nine formation 16, 55, 91
    Goose 155, 165
    Gypo Break 139, 149, 156, 165, 167
    Heart 46, 106
    Helix 29
    Kite 24, 29, 39
    Mirror Roll 30, 35, 39, 149, 163, 167
    Palm Tree split 16, 31, 135
    Phoenix Bend 39, 149, 152
    Phoenix pass 132, 134
    Python 127
    Rollback 68, 149
    Short Diamond 70
    Spaghetti Break 16, 135
    Steep Climb 155
    Swan 29, 75
    Synchro Crossover 46
    Synchro Split 135
    Vertical Break 39, 149, 155
    Vixen Break 127, 149
    Wine Glass 46
French, Sir Joe (Chief of the Air Staff) 48

Hackett, 'Willy' (Wg Cdr) 50
Hanna, Ray 44
Harrier 7, 23, 49, 59, 83
Hawk 11, 12, 20, 39, 43, 44, 45, 50, 53,
    55, 59, 73, 89, 92, 94, 96, 98, 99, 101,
    105, 109–123, 139, 143, 162, 163, 165

Hawker, Jas (Wg Cdr) 7, 9, 10, 11, 12, 20,
    50, 63, 64, 66, 67, 70, 83, 84, 143
Hawker Siddeley 109, 120
Heath, Mark 'Ted' (Cpl) 92
Heaton, 'Alfie' (Cpl) 94
HMS Illustrious 130
HRH The Duke of Edinburgh 43
HRH The Queen Mother 48
Hudson, Chris 44
Hurricane 50
Huxford, Rachel 56

In Season Practice (ISP) 11

Jaguar 7, 23, 55, 123
Jepson, Spike (Sqn Ldr) 48
Jet Provost T4 43
Jones, Lee (Flt Lt) 9, 43
Jones, Mark 'Flash' (Sgt) 92
Jones, Pete (Cpl) 143

Keith, Andrew 'Boomer' (Flt Lt) 54, 59,
    83, 101, 127, 132
King Hussein of Jordan 48

Lamb, Peter 'Lamby' (SAC) 128, 131,
    132, 134
Lewis, Gaz (SAC) 92, 100
Lightning 49
Lindsay, Ian (Sgt) 105
'Liney' 89, 91
Ling, Mike 'Lingy' (Flt Lt) 54, 63, 80, 83,
    128, 162, 165

Marks, Chris (Sgt) 90
Mason, Dunc (Sqn Ldr) 55
May, John (Warrant Officer) 96
McIlroy, Charlie (Flt Lt) 45
Miller, Simon (SAC) 143
Miniature Detonation Cord (MDC) 110,
    118, 162
Mirage 2000 48
Montenegro, David (Flt Lt) 72
Murphy, Ben 'Baz' (Sqn Ldr) 54, 80, 84,
    162
Murray, Alan (Adjutant Warrant Officer)
    143

Navigation Officer 136
Nicholson, Mick (Cpl) 104

O'Grady, Pablo (Flt Lt) 29, 80, 127
O'Keeffe, Liam (SAC) 96
Patounas, Dicky (Sqn Ldr) 59, 60
Perilleux, Greg (Flt Lt) 84, 129
'pigz' 128, 134, 136
Public Display Authority (PDA) 67, 83,
    90, 127
public relations 7, 24, 143

QE2 48
Quick Reaction Alert (QRA) 72

radio calls 11, 46, 70, 72, 160–161, 165
RAF Akrotiri, Cyprus 34, 48, 53, 55, 56,
    59, 62, 83, 84, 125, 127, 135
RAF Brize Norton 55, 56
RAF Cosford 90, 100
RAF Cranwell 24, 44, 66
RAF Fairford 43, 64
RAF Halton 100
RAF Leeming 109
RAF Leuchars 47, 55, 128, 131, 134
    Battle of Britain Airshow 43
RAF Marham 12
RAF Scampton 11, 34, 45, 54, 55, 59, 64,
    66, 73, 83, 84, 94, 98, 99, 105, 118,
    126, 139, 143
RAF Shawbury 75, 139
RAF Valley 43, 55, 64, 76, 109
RAF Waddington 50, 90
    Airshow 50
Rea, Simon 'Kermit' (Flt Lt) 54, 59, 63, 100
Red 1 (the 'Boss') 7, 11, 16, 20, 24, 29, 35,
    46, 53, 60, 61, 63, 66, 68, 70, 72, 75,
    76, 83, 84, 106, 107, 128, 131, 132,
    139, 147, 149, 152, 160, 161, 162
Reds 1–5 (Enid) 24, 29, 68, 80, 127, 131,
    149, 155, 160, 165
Red 2 24, 54, 61, 64, 72, 75, 76, 77, 100,
    152, 156, 161
Red 3 31, 61, 72, 75, 76, 128, 152, 161
Red 4 24, 39, 45, 61, 72, 76, 128, 131,
    156, 161
Red 5 31, 39, 76, 100, 101, 128, 131, 161
Red 6 (Synchro Leader) 24, 30, 35, 46, 80,
    128, 131, 139, 160, 162, 163
Reds 6 and 7 (Synchro Pair) 9, 12, 24, 25,
    39, 46, 80, 84, 149, 156, 157, 158, 159,
    167
Reds 6–9 (Gypo) 24, 29, 80, 83, 131, 139,

149, 155, 165
Red 7 29, 30, 34, 39, 46, 66, 76, 162, 163
Red 8 16, 30, 35, 39, 59, 83, 149, 152,
    155, 156, 159, 163, 167
Red 9 24, 31, 83, 132, 149, 152, 156, 167
Red 10 (Road Manager) 24, 29, 67, 125,
    127, 128, 132, 135
Red Pelicans 43
Roberts (SAC) 91
Roberts, Carl (Sgt) 96
Robins, Andy (Flt Lt) 29, 125, 127, 128,
    135
Rolls-Royce 50, 122–123
    Adour engine 105, 118, 122–123
Royal Air Force Aerobatic Team (RAFAT)
    7, 9, 10, 43, 50, 134
Royal Flying Corps 9
Royal International Air Tattoo 50, 64

Sennett, Zane (Flt Lt) 54, 64, 72, 75, 76, 77
Seward, Nick (Group Captain) 80
Slow, Dave (Flt Lt) 59
smoke 11, 23, 24, 34, 39, 46, 80, 83, 96,
    106, 107, 118, 130, 132, 147, 156, 158,
    159, 160, 165
Spitfire 50
Springhawk 59, 83, 99, 101, 125, 133
Stirrup, Sir Jock (Air Chief Marshal) 48
support team 10, 24, 89–107

Targett, Pete (Cpl) 94
Team Manager 24

Thomas, Emma 'Trigger' 131, 143
Thurley, Ade 46
Tornado 7, 12, 23, 59, 63, 72
Trott, Jon (Sqn Ldr) 143
Tucano T1 12, 109
Typhoon 59

van Koningsveld, E. J. 163

Wheeler, Rob (SAC) 98
winter training 55, 59, 66, 67, 72, 80, 83,
    91, 96
Wright, Dave (Cpl) 104
Wright, Nikki 143

Yellowjacks 43, 50